Dad,
    I thought that you would enjoy
this book.
    Always remember that - I love you!
            Love always -
                Kristen

COMMIES, CROOKS, GYPSIES, SPOOKS & POETS

ALSO BY JAN NOVAK

The Willys Dream Kit

The Grand Life

Turnaround (with Miloš Foreman)

THIRTEEN

BOOKS

OF PRAGUE

IN THE

YEAR

OF THE

GREAT

LICE

EPIDEMIC

COMMIES, CROOKS, GY

ES, SPOOKS & POETS

BY

JAN
NOVAK

STEERFORTH PRESS

SOUTH ROYALTON, VERMONT

For information about permission to reproduce selections
from this book, write to: Steerforth Press L.C., P.O. Box 70,
South Royalton, Vermont 05068.

"Family Hotel" was reprinted with permission from *Travel Holiday* magazine.
"Hard-working Guy" originally appeared in *Island* magazine.

Library of Congress Cataloging-in-Publication Data
Novak, Jan, 1953–
Commies, crooks, gypsies, spooks & poets : thirteen books of Prague
in the year of the Great Lice Epidemic / by Jan Novak.
p.   cm.
ISBN 1–883642–09–4
1. Prague (Czech Republic) — Civilization.
2. Prague (Czech Republic) — Description and travel.
3. Novak, Jan, 1953–   — Homes and haunts — Czech Republic — Prague.
4. Authors, Czech — Homes and haunts — Czech Republic — Prague.
5. Authors, American — Homes and haunts — Czech Republic — Prague.
I. Title. II. Title: Commies, crooks, gypsies, spooks and poets.
DB2622.N68   1995
943.71 2043— dc20   95–2977

Manufactured in the United States of America
First Printing

FOR ADAM & SONJA

CONTENTS

BOOK
OF THE
UNKNOWN

THE BIG UNKNOWN

In July of 1992, I packed up the wife and two kids and moved to Prague, then still the capital of the country of Czechoslovakia. We were leaving a white town house on a leafy street of Oak Park, Illinois, and stepping into the Big Yawning Slavic Polluted Dirty Communist Unknown.

The wife was Prague-born, but she had spent two thirds of her life in the States. I'd lived the first sixteen years of my life in Kolín, a small town outside of Prague. The nine-year-old Adam and the five-year-old Sonja were Bug's-Bunny-Quoting Skittles-Sucking Roller-Blading Neutered-Cat-and-a-Neutered-Dog-Petting Americans. "I don't want any crying, you guys, because it's not gonna make any difference," I told them as we departed, "I've just burned all the bridges behind us."

But the fact of the matter was that I'd only rented our three-floor sliver of a genteel sixteen-unit building for one year to a young couple with a complicated story. She was married, but her husband was studying at a downstate university and she couldn't handle living with her Mom anymore. He was her cousin who was moving in with her only so that her upper-class, clutching family would turn her loose.

"They look like street people to me," commented our nicest neighbor warily.

"They've put up the rent for three months," I explained.

I didn't know that there was another guy in the picture, a long-haired guy with an earring. I didn't know both the young men rode motorcycles. I didn't know that by the time we'd come back, the young woman would have a tattoo of a tear-drop-shaped cross under the hairline in the trough of her neck. I didn't know that she'd be getting a divorce and seeing a shrink.

We were not only stepping into the Unknown, we were leaving the Unknown too.

THE UNKNOWN BEHIND

Watching us prepare to leave for Europe — renting a storage room, pausing the phone number, packing and repacking suitcases, hauling bags to the garbage dumpster — the neighbors wanted to know what had possessed us to do this. "You're taking your kids into a war zone?" a bookkeeper had asked, confusing the late Czechoslovakia with the late Yugoslavia, a common mistake in our leafy suburb.

He was appalled, even though he read the same paper as we did and had probably seen the story of the nine-year-old boy who, only a few weeks earlier, had found a couple of handguns at home. This kid lived some three miles from our street, but on the wrong side of the tracks, in a tough neighborhood on the West Side of the Cold City of Chicago, and his was a front-page story. He happened to be a third-grader like my son Adam, so I could vividly imagine what followed when he decided to show off his find in school. Nine-year-olds knew how to showboat — on the morning he got the guns, this boy swaggered right down the middle of his street toting a pistol in each hand. Didn't he know the guns were loaded? Or was he just feeling too cool to think? Was he so full of himself it didn't even faze him when the school bus stopped right in front of him? Did he figure he had the drop on anybody at all?

The bus had just discharged its morning passengers by the school. It was driven by a dependable man in his thirties — you didn't put bus loads of children into the hands of some young gangbanger, but the driver lived in the neighborhood, he was streetwise, and he could tell this kid was holding real guns. He pulled up to him gently and sprung the passenger door open — did the third-grader just stand there shifting his weight from foot to foot? Or was he old enough to get that Who-You-Talkin'-To? You-Talkin'-To-Me? charge of power a gun could give you?

The bus driver had seen a lot of bizarre things on the streets: did he flash the kid a warm, fatherly grin? Did he start things off with a little small talk? Did he say, "Hey, what's happenin' . . . A nice little gun you got there, young man, real nice . . . See it a minute?"

Was the kid flattered to be treated as an equal by a grown-up? Did he just accept it as his due? Was it just another pretty color in that rainbow of emotion that a gun pumped you up with? He climbed into the open door. Did he step right up to the bus driver? Did he hang back at all? He handed the driver one of his guns. Was it the smaller one? Was he showing the older man he was no dummy?

The driver weighed the pistol in his hand, eyeballing the other gun. Did he go, "Oooh, that's bad, real bad . . . Now lemme see if the other one feel as good?" The driver was sitting down, so their eyes were on the same level, they both had a gun in their right hands now — they could have been equal, but both the guns belonged to the kid: he had the righteousness of ownership on his side, he was the more equal person. And he was streetwise too. What did he say? "Gimme my other gun back first"? Did he bother to say, "please," or "sir," or "mister"? Did those words always stick in his throat? Or did he sense that he would lose a little leverage by uttering them right then?

Did the driver chuckle and accept his less equal role? Did he return the small gun first, then try the grip on the bigger pistol? Did he treat the weapon as gingerly as he treated the kid? What did he say? "It's awright, but it ain't as good as the other one. Tell you what . . . I'll give you five bucks for this piece, kid . . ."?

The kid didn't know the gun was worth about one hundred and fifty dollars, but he knew a thing or two about distrusting people. Did he go, "Uh, uh! That ain't enough . . . That ain't nowhere near enough . . . You gotta gimme at least thirty dollars"?

Did the driver look disgusted? Did he say, "Man, you drivin' a hard bargain"? Did he just pull out his wallet and show it to the kid? Was there only a single banknote inside, a twenty-dollar bill? Were the twenty dollars in smaller bills? Did he get dramatic? Did he throw the wallet to the kid and say: "Now you gimme both of 'em guns and you can have all the bread in there"?

Twenty dollars was a lot of money to the third-grader, but not enough to give up both guns. Did the driver push the kid to sell both guns? Or did he try to wrap up the deal quickly, settling for what he could get? Was he concerned that somebody might see him closing this sale?

In the end, cautiously, the smaller gun and the money changed hands again — and that was that. The kid jumped off the school bus. He was the driver's business partner now; did he say good-bye to the man? Did he wave the loaded gun?

The driver shut the door and drove away. He had just picked up the world's easiest hundred bucks, which was all he'd had in mind.

The kid was happy with the deal too. He was not the greedy type. He headed to the corner store. Did he slip the loaded gun under his jacket? Did the cashier know him? Did the kid's shopping spree seem suspicious to her? Wasn't this boy usually just good for a lollipop, or a bubble gum? Where did he get the money to stack up all this chewing gum, these swizzles, licorice sticks, chocolate bars, chips on the counter?

Did the boy know how to beat the state sales tax? Did he have the cashier ring up each piece of candy separately? Two cents, two cents, a nickel, a dime, thirty-five cents? He walked out with a big old goodie bag. Did he spend all his money? Did he still have a bunch of change left to jangle in his pocket? Did he feel like a birthday boy? Did he dash to the school playground and make that feeling a reality? Did he show the gun to everybody? Did he pass out the candy? Was he everybody's buddy that morning? The candy bag was empty by the time the school bell rang, so the kid slipped his gun inside it and made for his class.

In third grade, you learned multiplication tables, you learned some simple geometry, you kept a writing journal. In the kid's class, the morning session often started with a dose of writing, because it helped the students to settle down. That morning though, nobody could keep their minds on their writing journal — the kid kept showboating, flashing the gun and pretending to shoot it, yet the haggard teacher didn't become aware of the firearm in her class-room till it discharged. It wasn't clear how that happened — did the kid point it and squeeze the trigger, as some of the third-graders said? Did the gun stay in the brown bag and go off by accident, as his parents said?

The bullet struck the girl who sat in front of the kid as she was bending down to a page in her writing journal. She was a lively nine-year-old, a good student. Did she wear a light blue dress? Did she gather her hair into a pony tail? Did she like to jump rope? The bullet hit her in the spine. She was paralyzed from the neck down — some mornings, my wife burst into tears just reading the *Chicago Tribune*.

In the neighborhood of the generous boy, the gun-dealing bus driver, and the paralyzed third-grader there towered high-rises where mothers put their children to sleep in bathtubs at night to keep them safe from stray bullets. In the two-flats around them, the sofas stood away from the windows for fear of drive-by-shooters.

Luckily, my third-grader was walking to school on a different planet, but it lay only a couple of minutes away if you floored the gas pedal — it was scary how cheap life had become in America, how fast the pathology was rising in the society, how fast the American civilization was losing its discontents. I thought that, if anything, we might need a good reason to come back from the Golden Romantic Baroque Peaceful Gun-free City of Prague.

SCARS

When I left Czechoslovakia in 1969, it had been my father's decision: I didn't know I was leaving the old country for good, never said good-bye to the place, and still had a scar on my heart from it — moving to Prague was going to give me a chance to see if some of that scar tissue couldn't be reattached to something there.

I was also curious to see what life was like in the city where Communism had just died with a whimper they called the Velvet Revolution, curious about the impending split of Czechoslovakia, curious to learn how my friends were coping with the U-turn of post-Communism, yet the bottom line for our decision was the mortgage.

I'd been living by my pen for the previous three years, but I was having a hard time paying the house note every month. Falling steadily behind and having to borrow money, I was beginning to wonder if I hadn't been suffering from delusions of grandeur when I'd decided that I could make an Average Suburban Living purely on my own terms, which was by writing.

Not that I had any fall-back options — somehow, I'd always known I'd be a writer. In 1969, when I was abruptly severed from my native language, I was furious with my father: I was sixteen years of age and thought that language was fate. I was scared that another country was going to wear out my Czech which was the only tool I could imagine for my vocation.

We wound up in Chicago, where, for the next dozen years, I clutched my native tongue. It was in Czech that I wrote my first book, *Striptease Chicago,* a collection of short stories about the Czech immigrants who were living around me. I wound up translating some of the stories into English, but it was a tedious job of regurgitating scenes, insights, and sentences I'd thought I was done with.

By the time the book came out in the early eighties, however, everybody in my dreams spoke English. Even when I dreamt the classic émigré dreams of being trapped in the old country — being locked out of our summer cottage and watched closely by some old professors who pretended not to know me — I found English was spoken there, yet I still couldn't work up enough nerve to write in the language.

In 1982, I was sitting down to write a novel in Czech when the sheer magnitude of the translating drudgery I was setting myself up for suddenly hit me — this was a fairly dramatic moment in my life: I was literally staring at a blank sheet in my typewriter with the first sentence of the book a sort of mumbling in my head. I decided to hold everything and think this through. I went and made a pot of tea and tried to imagine how that opening sentence would sound in English — the inchoate mumbling immediately became a flood of words: the sensation was as if I'd been driving with the hand brake on and suddenly released it. The book wrote itself. I called it *The Willys Dream Kit* and never wrote in Czech again.

My second, purely American novel, *The Grand Life,* was inspired by the Cyber Technomaniac Double-Speak of Corpo America, where I was putting my shoulder to the wheel at the time as a front-line supervisor in the computer room of an utility company.

Both books were published by major publishers, received flattering write-up and prizes, but didn't sell. I was then fired from my job, and started writing *Turnaround* with Miloš Forman. This autobiography of the Czech-born film director of *One Flew Over the Cuckoo's Nest* and *Amadeus* paid my bills for a couple of years, yet by the spring of 1992 I'd spent all the advances and the book wasn't going to bring any more money till it came out in Europe. I thought I'd weather the transition in Prague — the move to Europe was a way of shifting my mortgage grief onto someone else and postponing a hard look at my Delusions of Suburban Grandeur.

THE UNKNOWN WITHIN

The sweetest thing about a year in Prague was that our kids would learn Czech there. They were still young enough to pick up the language easily. We had been teaching them Czech in Chicago, but it was a losing battle, even though Adam had spoken nothing but Czech till he was almost four years old. (It had been necessary to teach him his future second language first: once they spoke English, the immigrant kids often didn't see any reason to learn the language spoken only by a few grown-ups around them, the language of authority, orders, reprimands, and shame.)

Adam was three and a half years old when Zdena started looking for a preschool for him. She went and saw a dozen nursery schools in the leafy suburb, but the only place that could handle a boy who had no English was the preschool of the local synagogue — they had kids speaking Hebrew, Spanish, and Rumanian there. The catch was that we weren't Jewish. (When I had to put down religion on some form, I opted for "Catholic," though I'd never gone to church nor did I believe in God.) In the end, Adam was accepted by the synagogue school, because they had a severe shortage of boys — a month later, he was expressing himself in long, fluid English sentences, for the language had been there inside him.

The day he started speaking English, however, he began to lose his Czech. I fought back — on the subway, I'd egg him on to say in Czech to a surly, overweight, scruffy-looking bruiser: "Hi, fatso . . ." Adam got a big kick out of it, got the conspiratorial value of speaking an obscure Slavic language, but the cheap thrill gradually wore off.

When Sonja was born, we pointed her toward Czech too, but this girl was different — she would go on to become an ice-hockey player on an all-boy traveling team — and when, at the age of three, she decided she was through with Czech, she pushed the whole family over into English.

I regretted my kids didn't have Czech to show them the world through the filter of a very different mentality. Adam and Sonja were Americans, of course, but I'd had terrifying glimpses of the void at the heart of the American identity, and thought Czech could maybe provide them with another way of placing themselves in the world — I'd been watching the news with them one day, a few months before we left for Prague, when an item about Israel came on and Sonja informed us: "That's where the Jewish people live." She had been going to the same preschool at the local synagogue as Adam and she'd come home and croon Hebrew songs about David, the king of Israel. In the den that afternoon, Adam informed his little sister: "That's us. We are Jewish."

"No, we're not Jewish!" she said, because she had been given the accurate scoop at the synagogue.

"Yeah, we are! Tell her, Dad," said Adam, so I set him straight. He was shocked and furious: "*What?!* We're not Jewish?! So what are we?"

I told him that we were Americans — but who were Americans? Americans were people mad with business and money, people who changed their names for career reasons, people who picked up and moved around the continent for a job, folks who made new friends at the drop of a hat and never looked back, men and women sometimes as interchangeable as computer boards, people lacking a strong sense of the places they called home or a firm social structure to measure their lives against . . .

Some Americans lived for God, some for pleasure, some for money, and some only for their pets. They lived in shredded families, Grandpa and Grandma a voice in the telephone, fuzzy cousins, disconnected, "I'm still on my second wife," a man once informed me proudly at a suburban cocktail party. And after twenty years in the country, we had started to fit the bill too — at times I'd feel we were tumbling straight into the Maw of the Terrifying Commerce-Crazy American Emptiness.

My children had only one grandparent in their lives — a doting Grandma, but she spoke a different language than they did. Their grandfather was living on the streets of Las Vegas, a manic-depressive refusing to take medication, because it wasn't he who needed the pills, it was the rest of the world. He was homeless and sometimes he called collect from jails. And their other grandparents, my in-laws, owned a lovely house in the suburbs of San Francisco, but they rented it out and lived out of a trailer, staying mostly in a state park in California, unplugged from the rest of the family — they had no telephone, no address: if someone were to murder them there, it would be weeks before we would know.

In the summer of 1992, giving the state of our family in America was like reading Allen Ginsberg's *Kaddish* — I figured that by moving to the old country for a year, we might slow down the growth of the unknown within.

THE UNKNOWN AHEAD

I was born in a Dear Medieval Industrial Polluted Provincial Town of Thirty Thousand Souls where all the people who wore denim knew all the other people who wore denim. It lay forty miles east of Prague which, for years, was a place where you sat through an interminable opera — four times at the National Theater there, with different school classes, I saw the same beige production of Smetana's *The Bartered Bride.*

Back then I didn't notice the Operatic Beauty of Baroque Prague and didn't care what was real and what was unreal in its surreal history — in my mind the city's Gory Legends blended seamlessly with the Raw Obscure Quirky Facts of its Fantastical History: Rabbi Loew the Wise Shem-Running Golem-Making Magus seemed no less a figment of imagination than John of Nepomuk the Odd Patron Saint of Prague and Bridges. But I was thrilled by the bustle of Wenceslas Square, the train stations, the soccer stadiums, the rare black or Oriental face you glimpsed among the bobbing heads of a shifting crowd, the movies, the *Big Beat* you could hear in its clubs, the armies of pretty girls.

Then came Chicago — I didn't see Prague for years and it grew faint in my memory. Eventually, with my American passport, I was able to visit the old country and acquire an Overseas Tourist Notion of Prague. I could clearly picture the breathtaking beauty of Prague, but my mental images of the city floated in a sea of white space and white noise: they had no weather, no foreground memories before them, no alcohol spin, no faces crowding in, no depth — in the summer of 1992, I still had only a post-card knowledge of Prague, and it had been a long time since I'd seen an opera.

GUIDE
BOOK
OF
PRAGUE

LOGIC OF BEAUTY

What makes a city? A river. And what makes a river? An old stone bridge. And what makes a bridge? Some hills to admire it from. And what makes the hills? A castle of ancient kings.

APPLIED LOGIC OF BEAUTY

Prague's massive Hradčany Castle overlooked the Charles Bridge on the Vltava River from the brow of a hill. It had once been ruled by the kings of Bohemia, but the kings took the losing side in the Reformation wars and their city was slowly reduced to a backwater of the Habsburg Empire.

At the start of this century, Prague was inhabited by Czechs, Germans, and Jews, but no one fought for it in the two world wars — the city wound up shut off from the world on the east side of the Iron Curtain. The forty years of Communism had wrapped its old core in hideous *sídliště*, the Socialist Realist "site areas" of prefab highrise *paneláky*, but the ancient Prague was still a poem of oxblood roofs, golden towers, crooked streets, Baroque houses, dancing-stone saints, soft-lighted gas lamps, cranberry-red street cars, snow-white swans, olive-green domes of churches soaring to heaven like hot air balloons, cobblestone squares turning into murky mirrors every time it rained, and the *Orloj*, the mechanical wonder of a clock whose grim reaper shook his scythe at you with every hour that passing was duly struck.

PRAGUE'S SAINT

In 1393, on the orders of King Wenceslas IV, one John of Nepomuk was flung off the Charles Bridge, supposedly because he refused to tell the king the secrets of his queen's confessions. When John's body hit the water, it was observed that five stars flashed out — "five tiny licks of bluish flame as when you flambé an omelette" was how the Italian Bohemist Angelo Ripellino later imagined it, but John drowned in spite of the miraculous marriage of fire and water and rotted in his grave till the early 1700s.

At that time, the Catholics sorely needed a native saint for the recently pacified, Reformationist Bohemia — on a Jesuit hunch, the body of John of Nepomuk was exhumed and a crowd of learned witnesses watched in shock as the doctors, scraping mildew and clay off John's bones, discovered a bright red tongue in the mouth of his skeleton — by God's grace, the honorable tongue that wouldn't violate the sanctity of his queen's confession was still slimy with saliva.

PRAGUE'S NAIVE GENIUS

Master Hanuš the clock-maker was the sort of Spectacular Analytical Thinker who could hold in his mind a set of gears, trains, and bells that took up a three-story tower wide enough to fit a squash court in. He recalled its every pinwheel, escapement, curve-spring, pallet, hammer, disk, dial, pin, roller, and tooth-wheel, yet he paid a harrowing price for his genius. His *Orloj* timepiece on the Old Town Square astounded the Medieval Era: it gave the day, the month, and the season even while it struck the hours and showed, in a tiny window in the *Orloj*'s face, a procession of the twelve apostles, a crowing rooster, and the grim reaper. The clock was called one of the Mechanical Wonders of the World — Master Hanuš took half a lifetime to construct it and, as soon as it was done, he lost all interest in it. In the end, as an afterthought, he gave it away to the King of Bohemia.

The greedy king was delighted with the spectacle chronometer — so delighted that he ordered that Master Hanuš's eyes be plucked out. The king's action had no personal dimension: he didn't care that his mind was no match to Master Hanuš's, but he was smart enough to do some Cold Feudal Calculation — if the genius of Master Hanuš were disabled, he correctly reasoned, then no one else in the world could ever possess an invention as sublime as his *Orloj*.

The loss of his eyes stunned Master Hanuš. He hadn't paid much attention to the ways of the political people and didn't know how the powerful used and discarded those around them. He was living in deep darkness now, but he was learning from it, acquiring the Socratic wisdom, learning to know himself. He finally understood that he had been drawn to the orderly, precision-ruled mechanical world because he had unconsciously striven to avoid dealing with the unpredictable ways of human beings. He also finally accepted the fact that you always lived in a messy human reality — you could never escape the brutality and the self-interest of others. He knew now that you had to confront it.

When Master Hanuš's eye sockets healed, he asked a small boy to lead him into the clock tower. He stood there for a long while and soaked up the hundreds of ticking motions his invention made. It was a percussive symphony of a heart-stopping beauty and he didn't regret composing it even though it had cost him his eyes. He longed for the quiet and dense music to play on forever. It soothed him so much he almost walked away again, but then he got hold of himself: he couldn't stop time, couldn't make the moment last forever, didn't even know if God could. He was an old blind man who could no longer afford sentimentality. He had to act on what he now knew about other people, about himself, and about his place in the world. He stood on his tiptoes and stuck his arm deep into the chronometer. He didn't grope around it, his touch was sure. He ripped out a few springs — all the ticking stopped and the *Orloj* stood still for the next hundred years.

PRAGUE'S NAIVE POLYHISTOR

The only man in Prague who could have fixed the *Orloj* was Doctor Faustus, but he didn't live in the same era. This scholar was as greedy as Master Hanuš's king — he had sold his soul to Mephistopheles to become a polyhistor, to possess the sum of all knowledge in the world.

Doctor Faustus owned a big house on the short side of Prague's Cattle Market where the municipal gallows stood. He lived there into a ripe old age, mostly buried in the books of his splendid library. But all good things had to come to an end, so one day Mephistopheles came to collect the soul the young Faustus had signed away in blood — suddenly, at the last minute, Faustus had a change of heart. Had he always intended to stiff Mephistopheles? Did he figure that, having all legal and philosophical knowledge at his fingertips, he would in the end find some way to break the contract? Or did he sign in blood thoughtlessly, with a young man's delusion of immortality? Did he think that thirty, forty, fifty years was the same as eternity? The fifty years went by like a dream; the contract was simply written and as solid as granite; Mephistopheles was all business as he knocked loudly and entered the cluttered study. His demeanor made it very clear that his time was valuable and there was nothing to talk about, yet the old man Faustus lost his composure: he started protesting and begging and pissing and moaning — Mephistopheles finally had to grab the polyhistor and fly away with him, but he was so disgusted with the doctor that he slammed him right through the ceiling. For many years, the House of Doctor Faustus had a gaping hole in its roof.

PRAGUE'S GRANITE

In the Kremlin, Iosif Djugashvilli was only four feet, eleven inches tall, but in Prague he had once stood 270 feet tall, a Socialist Realist Granite Generalissimo Leading the Red Army to Victory. (Stalin being the tallest man in the group sculpture, he was leading a Red Army of Midgets.) The Georgian Genius of Communism never even got to see himself on that scale, though — the whole project was a disaster of timing.

In 1949, Stalin celebrated his seventieth birthday and, in Moscow, they had to build a museum for all the lavish gifts pouring in from the four corners of the Earth. The greedy Czech comrades tried to outdo everyone else and sent word that, as their birthday gift, they would erect in Prague the tallest statue of Stalin the world had ever seen. They didn't fully realize, though, what a massive undertaking such a gigantic portrait in stone entailed: Stalin's statue wasn't actually finished until 1958 — five years after his death and two years after Nikita Khrushchev had denounced Stalin's mass murders and vanities, labeling them the Cult of Personality, a classic in the rich tradition of political euphemisms.

The granite Stalin was a political embarrassment even as he was unveiled, but four years later all the images of the Georgian Generalissimo became completely untenable. Yet, the Prague Communists didn't know how to blast the huge mass of stone out of the densely populated city. In the end, a capitalist firm had to be hired to dynamite the Supreme Communist into the Dust Bin of History: all Prague watched in fascination as German demolition experts decapitated Stalin and then took him down granite epaulet by granite epaulet. Most Czechs were amused, though some were heartbroken, and only the maker of the sculpture was spared the spectacle: he had committed suicide years earlier.

PRAGUE'S MUD

In the late Middle Ages, Rabbi Loew came to Prague's Jewish ghetto from the East, bringing with him a *shem* more powerful than dynamite — the coin-shaped charm containing the Name of the Unnameable probably could have been used to animate the granite Stalin and walk him out of the city if, hundreds of years earlier, Rabbi Loew hadn't found another use for his *shem*.

A shrewd reader of situations, the rabbi had summed up the wisdom of the Diaspora when he observed, "Nothing is the way it is . . ." Arriving in Prague, which for Jews had traditionally been one of Europe's more hospitable places, the rabbi argued that the inhabitants of its ghetto needed a strong guard to walk the maze of its streets at night and protect them. Did the rabbi once again see through appearances? Or was he being dramatic? Was he just a stranger seeking to make a quick impact on his new domicile? Was he paranoid? But wasn't a paranoid Jew a contradiction in terms in Europe?

Rabbi Loew didn't give anyone the time to ask these questions — one night, he made for the banks of the Vltava River, slapped together a colossus of mud, and managed to bring him to life by placing the *shem* with the Name of the Unnameable under his tongue. He called the creature the Golem, or the "man of clay" in Hebrew.

Rabbi Loew was a great Magus, but he was a lousy sculptor — his homunculus came out looking like a fat basketball center recovering from third-degree burns. The rabbi didn't care because nobody had to look at his man of clay. He kept the Golem hidden in the synagogue and revived him only at night, just before he would send him out into the streets. In the morning, he would always pull out the *shem* again, so the dim life flowed safely in and out of the monster.

But in Prague too nothing was the way it was and nothing worked the way it was supposed to work for long — Rabbi Loew's lovely daughter Abigail soon fell in love with the Golem. It wasn't clear why, but one morning not long after that, the rabbi failed to remove the *shem* from the Golem's head. Was Loew merely being the absent-minded Magus and scholar? Did he genuinely forget about the Golem? Or did he omit to disable the monster, because he had visions of misshapen grandchildren dancing before his eyes? But weren't the fathers the last to know about these things?

Be that as it may, the poor Golem suddenly found himself squinting into the light of day like a blinded owl. A strange fire was breathing down on him from the brilliant sky, the shuttered houses suddenly had eyes and mouths as windows and doors started banging away around him, the deserted streets began filling up with throngs of people of all odd sizes: the nocturnal Golem had never even seen children before, had never known the world held so many people, so many carts and wagons, so many carriages. Before this day, he had watched rats, cats, and dogs howling at the moon. He may have glimpsed an incubus or a succubus here and there, and perhaps he had even heard an early rooster crow, but now he was trapped in a confusion of noisy people, horses, oxen, dogs, goats, geese, hens, pigeons, sparrows, squirrels, a bear with a ring through his nose . . . He was used to the ample space of the night, but now the city had shrunk around him and he was reeling in a hot, bustling, noisy, scurrying madhouse — a ragman's cart bumped into him, he grabbed and flipped it over, a dog barked, he smashed it against a wall, the release of that gesture made him feel a little better, the dog's owner screamed, he hurled the man after the dog, he stomped on a potter's wares, took out a neighing horse with one punch, broke a gate, hurled a clay pot at the sun trying to knock it off the sky.

The only person who could save the ghetto from the rampaging monster now was Abigail — Rabbi Loew ordered his daughter to go and remove the *shem* from under the Golem's tongue, betraying the fact that he had known about her romance all along.

When the Golem saw Abigail approaching, he froze — the young woman was the only person who could have transported him out of his fearful frenzy. She obeyed her father and walked up to the monster. She kissed him: she kissed the Golem as tenderly as she could, kissed him choking on tears, kissed him gasping for breath, kissed him hurting terribly, kissed him because this was what she had been longing to do, though not before her father, not in public, not in the light of day. She kissed the monster to show him her love, kissed him to show her father how she loved the Golem, kissed him to show it to the whole world, and she kissed him to kill him. She killed him to save her father, killed him to make up for her father's pride and thoughtlessness, killed him so that she wouldn't commit incest because her father was also the Golem's father.

The Golem was happy. If Abigail wanted to kill him, he wanted to die. His whole dim life was easily worth this fleeting sweetness, this brief delight of lips pressing together, breaths mingling, tongues sliding over each other passionately, bodies promising to grow into one, the whole world watching, the whole world falling away . . .

Abigail the good girl till the bitter end did as her father had told her — with her tongue she scooped the *shem* out the Golem's mouth. At that moment, the Golem collapsed and Abigail ended up lying under a heap of river mud. Was she ever able to wash off the mud that was her brother, her love? Or was she smeared with it forever? Did she ever get over the Golem? Did she spit out the *shem*? Did she swallow it? Did she choke on it? Was her act a murder-suicide, a noble murder and a delayed suicide? Wasn't anything in Prague the way it was?

PRAGUE'S IMAGINATION

In the fall of 1989, Martin Šmíd died for the Velvet Revolution that ended Communism in Prague and brought the playwright Václav Havel to power. A mathematics major at the Charles University, Šmíd was its only victim when he succumbed to the injuries sustained during a student demonstration — the news that a young man had been clubbed to death caused the smoldering political revolt in Prague finally to catch fire, enraging the city and giving heart to its timid fence-sitters. Candlelit altars to the memory of Martin Šmíd's martyrdom quickly sprung up on many corners in the center of Prague, but they seemed strangely incomplete: they were all lacking a photograph of the martyr.

A frantic search failed to turn up not only any photographs of Martin Šmíd, but also his remains. In the confusion of the student riot, many eyewitnesses had seen a limp body lying on the cobblestones, had watched it being covered with a white sheet and carried off to an ambulance, yet when the searchers combed the hospitals and the morgues of the city for the body of the revolution's martyr, they found nothing. No grieving relatives, no sobbing girlfriend ever stepped forth and, in the end, it was established that the Charles University had no record of a Martin Šmíd — the dead revolutionary whom so many people had so clearly seen through the veils of tear gas was an imaginary being.

Theories abounded, but it was never satisfactorily explained whose nefarious purposes the Imaginary Corpse of Revolutionary Prague had served. Martin Šmíd had sparked the Velvet Revolution, but had he been a figment of misinformation by the Soviet KGB? The Czech *STB*, the State Security? A tool of obscure power struggles in the expiring Communist party? Would the revolution have happened without him? Could he possibly have been a cynical ploy of Czech dissent? Or had Martin Šmíd simply been the Pure Immaculate Issue of Prague's *Genius Loci?*

PRAGUE'S BLUE BLOOD

The Habsburg emperor Rudolph II had been Prague's last royalty. This contemporary of Rabbi Loew wore the crown of the Roman

Empire, but he neglected the affairs of government to work with wood-carving tools, weaver's looms, and oil paints. A manic-depressive, he kept diplomatic envoys waiting for months on end while he hung out with astrologers, alchemists, and purveyors of philosopher's stones and kits that transmuted iron into gold. He supported an army of artists, madmen, and con men, amassed a staggering collection of artifacts and curiosities, and left a huge imprint on the Prague imagination.

Rudolph II brought to Prague the astronomers Johann Kepler and Tycho Brahe who was said to have died of a burst bladder — he was afraid to rise from the imperial table before the brooding emperor did. Tycho Brahe wore a golden prosthesis in place of a nose he had lost in a duel and his strange face may have inspired Rudolph's court painter to develop his fantasist style: when Giuseppe Arcimboldo painted the face of a librarian, it was made of books; he drew the imperial cook as a heap of pots and pans; he constructed faces out of bouquets of flowers. His sitters had to view themselves as intricate arrangements of birds and hunting animals, fruits and vegetables, candles and fire-tools, arms and war instruments, bottles and wineglasses, trees and lichens, fish and toads and sea critters, for, in Prague, every portrait was a metaphor.

INDEX

Prague was the place where Wolfgang Amadeus Mozart composed music, Albert Einstein taught physics, Franz Kafka adjudicated insurance claims, Rainer Maria Rilke wore the dresses of his dead sister, Jaroslav Hašek stole dogs, and Jaroslav Seifert stole kisses.

BOOK
OF THE
INVISIBLE
HAND

TAG-TEAM RAP QUARTETS

Prague suffered from a chronic housing shortage and new arrivals had to scramble to find a place to stay, but we were in luck. Mirek Ondříček, the cinematographer of Miloš Forman, Lindsey Anderson, and Penny Marshall, had a small apartment in the center of the city lined up for us. We moved our twelve pieces of luggage into a six-story Art-Nouveau building on *Francouzská* Street of Prague's *Vinohrady* district, and the good news was that our apartment there had a black rotary phone. The bad news was that the phone line was shared by nine other subscribers — if one of them was using the telephone, the other eight receivers were dead. Now the subsidiary good news was that most of the people sharing the line were old pensioners — they didn't use their phones a lot because it was expensive. The subsidiary bad news was that some of our elderly neighbors were reclusive — if they didn't want to be bothered with the world, they simply took their phone off the hook. At one point, we had no dial tone for two weeks straight.

Even when you did get the dial tone, phone calls were difficult in Prague. You'd dial and, more often than not, there would be only the hypnotic sound of distance, a periodic click, a humming wire, so you had to dial again. When you did get through, it was common to have another conversation whispering in the background as a kind of anthropological static. Often you could hear the other people better than your own interlocutor. In that case, the protocol dictated that those who got grafted onto the original conversation were supposed to hang up and dial again, but some rude callers stayed on and turned the call into a tag-team rap quartet. At the end of the month, the phone bill arrived in the mail. It showed no breakdown of charges, stating only the period covered and the amount owed.

In the summer of 1992, John Bok, a Phenom of Czech Dissent and Václav Havel's Body Guarding Shadow during the Velvet Revolution, received a phone bill for over five thousand crowns. At the time, he was still the Deputy Director in the Office for the Protection of Constitution and Democracy of the Czech Ministry of Interior but his paycheck didn't cover it — not that John Bok was going to pay the bill anyway. "The fuckin' numbers were sheer fantasy! We weren't even home for most of that month! We were on vacation!" he told me with his customary passion, "I never had a phone bill like that in my goddamn life!" He called the phone company for an explanation, but its clerk wouldn't even discuss the numbers: "Look, either you pay in full, or we terminate your service."

Bok liked nothing better than a fight, but he tried to hold himself back: "Sir, I'm sorry, but you people just have got to give me a little more to go on here ..."

"No, we don't," said the phone company clerk. "And you'd better pay, or you won't have a phone."

At that point, John Bok lost it. He ranted and raved and didn't pay. His phone was cut off. He left the Ministry of Interior and, finally, started making good money by cleaning the men's room of an American-owned night club in Prague called Radost — such was the Roller Coaster of Revolutionary Fortunes in the Land. There was a small fee for using the toilet which went to the attendant: John Bok kept his shells sparkling clean and, shrewdly, he taped a photograph of himself shaking hands with President Bush on his gleaming tiles. It was a memento from the days when he had been close to the center of power — on a good weekend night, when the club was crowded with drunken Americans, Bok cleared more as "a john hag" than he had in a week at the Ministry of Interior, so he finally went ahead and paid the outrageous phone bill, just to have the service restored. And then he sued. The last I heard the case was still in litigation.

ADVENT OF STRESS

By the time we got to Prague, nearly three years had elapsed since the Late Anemic Communism in the country had expired and Czechoslovakia was now run by a Chicago-school economist. Its newspapers and its politicians were full of New Capitalist Concepts, such as free market economy, conversion from the closed to an open system, privatization, return to Europe, the invisible hand of the market — I resolved to see if these terms were just fancy buzzwords, or if they could be taken seriously: I'd go out and buy a domestic Škoda automobile.

The Czech cars were cheap which was good for our tight budget, and we were the Post-Modern Americans Abroad: we figured that by having the same wheels as the other people in Prague, we could better partake in their existential experience. But when I asked an uncle where you went to buy a Škoda in Prague, he told me proudly that there was now a brand new Maserati dealership in *Žižkov*, a Peugeot dealer at the top of Wenceslas Square, an Alfa Romeo lot in *Smíchov*, a Porsche dealer in . . .

"Yes, but I'm in the market for a Škoda," I interrupted him.

"*You* don't want a Škoda," he said even though he was a Škoda owner himself, "being an American and all . . ."

"But I do."

"Well, I read that they've got Škoda dealerships in Jerusalem and Istanbul, but here everybody buys 'em straight from the factory in Mladá Boleslav," he informed me irritably.

For the previous forty years, there had been no need for car dealers in the country: the Communist government had printed piles of Czechoslovak crowns while making few Škodas, so the money had been furiously chasing the cars. The car-buyers paid a deposit, got their name on a list, and waited for a few years. One day, they were finally told to show up at a garage. A mechanic would drive up in their Spanking-New Lifetime-Of-Saving Pride-Of-Possession Škoda Baby, and the suspense was over — they finally saw what color they'd drawn in the Happy Lottery of Socialist Shopping.

How did that feel? I asked my uncle. Could you even call this demeaning enterprise shopping? How impotent can a consumer get, right?

"It was kinda nice, actually," the uncle shrugged his shoulders, "you didn't have to make any choices, so you couldn't screw up. Now you've got to make up your own mind about every damn thing and thinking hurts. Not only that, you can get the wrong stuff and there's no one to blame it on. Back in the old days, if you had any luck at all, there'd be something wrong with the car they gave you — the color was hideous or the windows rattled or something — so you got to bitch about the goddamn government to your heart's content . . . I used to sleep like a baby at night."

In Czechoslovakia, the End of Communist Rule marked the Advent of Stress.

PARADOX OF HISTORY

The Škoda dealership was easy to overlook. It lay on a desolate thoroughfare on the eastern periphery of Prague and there was no showroom, just five dusty automobiles on a patch of gravel, surrounded by a chain-link fence. A small sign tacked onto a street lamp pointed to a Volkswagen garage to which the dealership was merely a sideshow, because the Volkswagen Company now owned the majority stake in the Škoda Works. (The Germans had bought it when the Czech government began its *privatizace* or its sale of the state-owned companies. There had been other bids for Škoda, submitted by French and American carmakers, but the Germans promised to keep the Škoda name and to supply the cars with modern technology.)

Volkswagen's acquisition of Škoda was itself a paradox of Central European history: Škoda was the older, more storied carmaker — you had it all there in the name: Emil von Škoda was an engineering genius who had set up vast manufacturing works in the city of Plzeň and his car's name harked back to the days of Mr. Daimler, Mr. Peugeot, Mr. Ford and Mr. Bugatti. Volkswagen, "the people's wagon," belonged to the modern age of the concept — it had begun with Adolph Hitler's populist idea that the German masses deserved an affordable car.

You would never know it from looking at the Škodas now, but between the wars, Plzeň's automobiles competed for the European market with Stuttgart's Mercedes-Benzes. Then, in 1948, the Communists took power in Czechoslovakia and, for four decades, the technological development in the country froze. By the summer of 1992, Škodas lagged so far behind their Western counterparts that the only Detroit descriptive that applied to them was "a little shitbox." In the age of the jelly-bean look, the Škodas had a boxy shape and a plastic interior. They came in five colors and there were as many Škodas on the streets of Prague as there were cabs in Manhattan.

The carmaker claimed that it produced two models of Škodas, but they were clearly making just one car — from the front, you couldn't tell the difference between their puny station wagon, called Škoda *Forman*, which cost a little over six thousand dollars, and their five-door sedan, called Škoda *Favorit*, which was a foot shorter and came out to some four and a half grand.

The cheaper *Favorit* was what I was looking for, but all I saw on the sun-beaten gravel patch of the dealership were the *Forman* station wagons, locked and covered with a thick layer of dust. The sales office inside the Volkswagen garage was a Blast from the Socialist Past: veils of cigarette smoke; a middle-aged Empress lording it over an orderly line of Humble Supplicants; a bench with a Smiling Eternal Observer who was waiting to bribe or brownnose someone . . . The Czechs entered all offices on cat's feet, but I was an American.

"Excuse me, is this where I'd buy a *Favorit?*" I asked the Empress loudly. I don't have a foreign accent in Czech, so for a beat she peered at me as if I might be pulling her leg — I realized there were no *Favorits* to be had and that I was supposed to know that.

"I don't have any *Favorits*," she finally said. "Nobody has them."

"All right, so when are you gonna get some?"

"I'm not getting anymore cars this month," she shrugged her shoulders. "And then the factory goes on vacation. Come back toward the end of the summer."

The End of Communism, it seemed, didn't put an end to the Communist Thinking: there was a heavy demand for *Favorits*, yet the Škoda Works weren't hiring people, adding shifts, and increasing production — the factory was shutting down for a company holiday. Where the hell was the Invisible Hand of the Car Market?

I called the Škoda plant in Mladá Boleslav and was switched to a sales coordinator: "We should have a car for you no later than January . . ."

"Wait a minute! You're telling me you've got a waiting list half-a-year long and you're *shutting down* for a couple of weeks?"

"Well . . . But this is nothing new!" the coordinator saw my point at least and grew defensive. "We've been doing that ever since I've been here . . ."

"Yes, but you're working for the Germans now, aren't you? And I always thought that at least they were in the business to make money."

But then, in the course of the pointless argument, it hit me: maybe the fewer *Favorits* they produced, the more money the Germans made — weren't Volkswagen and Škoda natural competitors? Didn't they both go after the same, low-end of the car market? And hadn't the cheap Škodas been beating out the fancier Volkswagens in a number of countries, such as Israel, Turkey, and the whole of Eastern Europe? And wouldn't the purchase of the Škoda Works give the Volkswagen executives the perfect means to rectify this? They could now keep the production of Škodas deliberately low and nudge some buyers toward their Volkswagens; they could also slowly improve the Škodas, increase their price, and kill off the demand for them completely. (The Germans didn't need to raise the price by much — the cost of the *Formans* was already high enough to discourage buyers.)

Over my year in Prague, the price of *Favorits* went up three times while their production never managed to catch up with the demand — if there was an invisible hand working the car market in Czechoslovakia, it was probably German and it was jerking off the Škoda automakers.

THE WAY OF THE GLOBE

It gradually became clear that, if I wanted to drive, I'd have to settle for a used *Favorit*. By then I'd been in the country a few weeks, long enough to recognize that to get anything done in Czechoslovakia, you still had to lean on friends and family, so I wound up back in the place where I was born.

The *Favorit* I came to see in the Provincial Town of Thirty Thousand Souls was supposed to be a Practically New Automobile while its owner was a Brand New Entrepreneur. He had a bricklayer's physique: thick fingers, a shock of thick gray hair, and a big gut, but he talked fast. His favorite subject was himself and he refused to show me the car until I had lunch with him.

We were strolling through the dining room of an unpretentious restaurant which he called his "personal canteen" when the entrepreneur stopped by the table of some guy in a suit. He stared at the guy for a beat — hard, without a trace of smile on his face — then grabbed his tab and walked on. It was an aggressive gesture, but the guy picked up his half-eaten plate of soup and followed his tab to our table. He didn't say anything. He smiled sheepishly as he pulled out a chair to join us.

"That seat's taken!" barked the entrepreneur, still stone-faced — this, I realized, was his idea of humor.

"That's correct, sir, it certainly is taken now," retorted the soft-spoken guy lamely.

He turned out to be the town's lawyer, who worked out of the city hall, and the entrepreneur wound up paying for his lunch — the lawyer never bothered to make even a perfunctory attempt to pick up his tab, but he certainly earned his food: he paid for it through his ears. For half an hour, obsequiously, he had to listen to the entrepreneur sing his Booming Song of the Self, yet the economics of this transaction were intricate and, on that day, spurred by my presence, the entrepreneur may have gone too far, for at the end of the lunch the lawyer suddenly asked the waitress for a pack of cigarettes. She jotted the modest price of the Czech cigarettes right on the entrepreneur's tab, for everyone there was clear on who was paying the lawyer's bill.

The entrepreneur said nothing. He watched her pen, watched her walk away, and then he called her back and pointedly changed the order: "Make that *a carton of Camels!*"

Now it was the lawyer's turn to be shocked: "No, no, no, wait a minute . . . I couldn't possibly . . ."

The entrepreneur waved off the objections and slapped the carton of Camels down before the lawyer — again there was no communication, no smiling, no small talk, there was only the high drama of the entrepreneur's naked contempt. It ended only when the squirming lawyer picked up the carton and headed back to the city hall, squeezing it under his arm as if it were a giant thermometer.

We watched him go. "Guess what, I never stand in any lines in this town," chortled the entrepreneur and then he Explained It All to me: "What is business? Business is who you know and what you can get out of it. I'm sure that in America, it's no different."

NO CRAZY GENTLEMAN

The entrepreneur was clear on the Way of the Entire Globe and he was in fine shape in such a world: the post-Communist mayor of the Provincial Town of Thirty Thousand Souls was a friend. And the entrepreneur's company had just bought a car for the town's police department too — "you gotta oil the wheels if you want 'em to run smooth for you . . ."

"But how did you get started in business in the first place?" I asked him.

He proudly told me the story. (It's background was that, for forty years, Czechoslovakia had been a one-company town. The Communists had owned the entire economy, so after the Velvet Revolution the Post-Communist government scrambled to shift all the enterprises in the country into private hands. Some businesses had been "nationalized" by the Communists in the forties, and these were simply returned back to the old owners or their heirs. But many business were not claimed by anyone — their owners had died or disappeared, or the enterprise had been started under Communism — and such assets were sold to private investors in "privatization auctions," which were held by the local governments in every town in the country.)

In the Provincial Town, the entrepreneur got together with three other partners to buy the town's public baths, a deal which also included a huge cleaner's in the basement. One of the partners had managed this cleaner's under the Communists, so they had the drop on all the other would-be capitalists in town.

"But I thought that these auctions were clean . . ." I said.

"Sure! The auction was on the up and up! Absolutely!" the entrepreneur told me, "the trick had been to keep the baths and the cleaner's as one entity for the auction . . ."

It was here that the entrepreneur's connections decided the issue — that decision was made by the local government people, and, under the entrepreneur's guidance, they went ahead and decided right against the town's best interest: the town would have made more money if the two enterprises had been split up for the auction. Separately, the baths and the cleaner's would have commanded more bids and brought in more money, but "that's where we licked them. It wasn't easy, but we kept it a single ball of wax . . ."

You needed more capital to bid on the whole building and its assets — no one else had that kind of money or the will to risk it, so the entrepreneur and his partners submitted a minimal bid and got the baths and the cleaner's cheaply. They were now washing the linen for most of the hospitals, schools, hotels, and other institutions in the area, though they had kept only the lucrative accounts — "some of these hospitals don't have any money and we ain't a charity . . ."

The entrepreneur, however, didn't have the patience to nurture a business. Running the cleaner's, he said, "was a pain in the ass." People couldn't be trusted: "Just yesterday, we caught our best employee, and she's a really hard-working lady . . . Dependable, always there, you name it . . . Well, we caught her with a box of detergent in her bag. What're you gonna do? I fire her and I shoot myself in the foot, so we went: boo boo boo! And that was it . . ." He hadn't lost his perspective on what it took to make a living with your hands in the Provincial Town: "For the money that we pay, we're lucky we can get anybody to work at the cleaner's at all. Hell, we can't all get rich on the damn cleaner's, it's not that big of a moneymaker."

The entrepreneur intended to get rich by cutting his costs — the partners closed the public baths "for renovation" shortly after they had acquired them. They boarded up the small pool and the hot and cold water dips where I'd once gone swimming as a kid. They ripped out the rich-smelling changing cabins where, through a knothole, I'd caught my first breathless glimpses of girl's pubic hair. And they were about to open a kind of a flea market in the old baths, where the sellers would rent stalls from the partnership. "There's big money in that because everyone's buying secondhand things these days — people just can't afford anything new around here."

The openness with which the entrepreneur was sketching his bilking schemes for me seemed surreal. As surreal as the naiveté of the town's politicians. "Hadn't the mayor seen this coming?" I asked, "Didn't he realize that you might close the public baths?"

"He realized it all right," said the entrepreneur. "He made us promise him that we would keep the baths running. We even shook our hands on it." He let out a big laugh. "Called it a gentleman's agreement . . ."

"But then you're not much of a gentleman . . ." I said, and for the first time during our conversation, the entrepreneur bristled: "Gentleman, gentleman . . . Hell, we're businessmen, all right? Everybody wants to be a gentleman, but we can't afford to be gentlemen! You lose your shirt on the goddamn baths! You get the old biddies splashing around the hot pool all afternoon, your energy bill is outta this world, but try charging her more than six crowns. Oh, boy! They'd eat you alive . . . So I told the mayor, I says, 'Okay, the town wants us to run the public baths? Fine! Then give us a subsidy! But I'm not paying for these people to sit in the goddamn sauna! Let the town pay for their sweat!' Gentleman, my ass! What am I, crazy?"

The entrepreneur wasn't a Crazy Gentleman and he wasn't a Crazy Business Partner: only three of the four original investors now remained in the company. One partner had been quickly squeezed out of the group — "that guy was a loser" — and, with his sole good-guy partner, the entrepreneur was scheming to get rid of the third man — "that guy is a bum."

The entrepreneur and his Non-Loser Non-Bum Partner had big plans. They had bought a ski lodge in the mountains. They were just about finished rehabbing it — "we're roasting a pig there in a couple of weeks, you can come and watch anybody who's anybody in this town stuff their faces there . . ." Then, in the winter, the mayor was going to take his kid there and "do a little complimentary skiing on our slopes . . ."

But this newest acquisition of the entrepreneur was not only a fancy tool for "oiling the wheels" of government. It had a solid bottom line too: "The area is full of Germans and they pay in D-Marks, so the lodge will be a big moneymaker for us . . ."

The restaurant was nearly empty by then, the lunch rush over. We had eaten the four courses of the traditional Czech lunch and the entrepreneur had downed five or six beers. His small eyes were glassy, but he had gotten even more intoxicated on the sense of his own cleverness: "We just bought a snow tractor for the lodge too. A real beauty. Made in Germany, a true blue Kassbohrer . . ."

The brand new snow tractor was worth over two million crowns, but the partners had bought it from a state company for under a hundred thousand crowns. "Well, we slipped the guy who signed off on the deal another couple hundred grand under the table, but it still was a steal . . ."

"But won't this person get into trouble?"

"Oh, no, he quit there already . . ."

"Yeah, but won't they come after him? You can't just give away stuff at a fraction of its value, can you?"

"Nobody cares, it's all state property anyway. They're giving it away everywhere you look and everybody's trying to grab a piece of the action . . ."

And so the buzzwords in the newspapers and in the mouths of the politicians were just that — buzzwords. In the provinces of the land, something else was happening entirely. It had nothing to do with a conversion from a closed to an open system, it was the Old Grab, it was about who could rip off more of what was being given away in Czechoslovakia.

The entrepreneur didn't believe that you got ahead in business by making something better or providing a more efficient service. His success rested almost entirely on exploiting his connections to the powerful. But he was not very smooth at "oiling the wheels" — he had humiliated the lawyer with the petty bribe — and he was careless with the results. He had no qualms about breaking his word to the mayor, "couldn't afford to be a gentleman" — it hadn't even occurred to him that corruption too was founded on trust.

From this man, I bought a used car.

THE BEST MONEY CAN BUY

The white *Favorit* was the Provincial Town's idea of glamour and it was loaded. This four-door hatchback sedan Škoda 136 L had a sunroof, fancy hubcaps, a tape deck, a filigreed Deco sunscreen, black Deco stripes, Deco ribs on the wipers, Deco gizmos on the doors, and a bright green Deco teardrop splattering on the front bumper. There were fuzzy seat covers of imitation leopard skin, rubber mats, and a square yard of cherry-sized wooden balls covering the driver's seat. (I never got the hang of this popular accessory of the Czech car culture — it was supposed to give you a kind of a massage while you drove, but I tore it out after ten minutes of sitting on it: my haunches were as sore and pock-marked as if I'd been sitting on a wooden door mat.)

The entrepreneur had owned the car for two years, but had only put eight thousand kilometers on it. "I've got an old Russian Zhiguli beater to get around in," he explained, "I kept this baby just to drive my daughter to the Conservatory."

Until recently, his daughter had been studying the flute at the conservatory in Brno, some hundred and fifty kilometers east of the Provincial Town. "She gave up her music now. The problem was that she was a virgin too long," the entrepreneur explained with his vintage surreal coarse openness, which was startling in that country of guarded people. "And that was probably my fault too, I was real strict with her and then she discovered cock: game, set, match . . . She was over twenty by then and it completely knocked her for a loop. She quit her studies. Probably hasn't touched the damn flute in months."

The entrepreneur's daughter fell hard for a man of unorthodox beliefs and married him over her father's wishes: "He's a goddamn bum, he won't ever amount to anything. The two of 'em go to church, they don't eat meat, they don't have a TV in the house — it's like I don't have a daughter anymore . . . I hardly ever see her anymore, so fuck it! I'm selling this car . . . I kept it just for her."

When, at long last, I was driving away from him in the best *Favorit* money could buy, the entrepreneur still ran after me, screaming, his big gut shaking like jelly: "Don't wait to shift, don't let the engine roar like that! Jesus Christ! You gotta shift sooner! She should be revved at twenty-nine hundred on the expressway!" My money was safely in his pocket, but he couldn't help himself. "And get theft insurance first thing! In Prague, fifty of 'em walk every day!"

SEVEN LITTLE WHITE CARS

The top-of-the-line Škoda *Favorit* had its quirks: if you wanted to put air in the tire, you had to pry the hubcap off; the gas gauge didn't work, so you had to zero out the auxiliary odometer every time you got gas; on hot days, if the tank was nearly empty and you unscrewed its cap, the gas tended to shoot out and spray you; if you needed a tune-up, you had to get up at six in the morning and drive for an hour to some Small Provincial Town, because no one trusted the repair shops of Prague — owning a Škoda certainly helped us try the Czech life on for size, but there came a moment when having a *Favorit* paid off in a very unexpected way.

In the first week of April of 1993, my best friend Geoff flew in from Chicago to help us celebrate my fortieth birthday and he stayed with us for a wild week. We talked and drank till dawn every night — the kids would give us good night while we were sitting at the kitchen table, they'd go to bed and dream of great fires and raging seas and frogs and princesses and witches with teacher's faces and horses and swans and elephants and skating on water, they'd dream till the daylight crept back into their room and woke them up and they'd stumble back into the kitchen, still warm and slow with sleep, and we would still be sitting at the kitchen table, now cluttered with empty bottles, and they'd say good morning to us and go off to school, and we'd have a nightcap and go catch a little shut-eye.

One morning late in that week, I was all partied out and called it a night at four o'clock. Geoff didn't mind, but he wasn't ready for bed yet. "Can I borrow your car?" he asked me. He was going to drive around and find himself a nice bar. All he wanted from life were two fingers of whiskey in a tall glass, a few ice cubes, and maybe a fat cigar. If he could find a chair by a big window where he could watch the streetcars rumble by, he could be a happy man.

His request didn't make me very happy: the Czech police were tough on drunk driving and Geoff's speech was slurred, his eyes were bloodshot, he spoke no Czech, and he didn't know the city, but while I knew all that, I also knew that there was no arguing with him. And I didn't want to come across as a petit bourgeois either, so I threw Geoff the keys and staggered off to bed.

I couldn't sleep though. I thought that there was good chance that Geoff might wind up in jail or a hospital or worse, and it was all my fault. But then, as I lay in bed reproaching myself, I heard Geoff stumbling back up the stairs. He couldn't get the key into the keyhole, so I went and opened the door for him.

Geoff stood there smoking a cigar and grinning from ear to ear. He threw me the keys: "Thanks, man . . ."

"Why? What happened?"

"Hell, there're seven of those little white cars you got on this goddamn block alone . . ."

"That's cool," I said. "Hell, I'll even drink to that."

"You're on," said Geoff and we went into the kitchen and opened a couple of beers and waited for everyone to wake up.

GRAVY

The Škoda failed us only once. In the winter of 1993, we were driving back to Prague from a week of skiing in the rocky, soaring High Tatras of Slovakia, where the car had stood by the hotel for several freezing nights. And after we'd stopped for a lunch at a Western-style Motor Rest near Brno, the *Favorit* wouldn't start. It had died in the perfect spot, though, right under a billboard which said: TOWING SERVICE — call Mr. Mašek.

My call was answered by a gruff voice: "Mašek here."

I said I needed a jump and Mašek hung up on me: "You can kiss my ass with piddley crap like that!" he'd growled.

Mr. Mašek was a pretty droll sort of business owner — I had to laugh as I went to see if I could get some respect for my problem from the Motor Rest people. The manager there was a very busy man and, as soon as he understood what my problem was, he reached for a telephone and dialed a number. He mumbled something into the receiver, mutely handed it over to me, and I heard a pleasant, sing-song voice: "Hello, Mašek here."

"Well, I already know what I can do with my piddley crap, Mr. Mašek," I said, "but the fact is, I still need a jump . . ."

Mr. Mašek couldn't hang up on me now — he would have in effect been hanging up on the Big Tuna of the Motor Rest. He choked on embarrassment for a beat, then proceeded to geeee and aaaaah. "Well, why don't you get somebody to give you a push like everybody else?" he finally spat out what he had in mind.

"Mr. Mašek, do you have a towing service or don't you have a towing service? Maybe you shouldn't put up any billboards when you don't want to be bothered by customers . . ."

"I'll be there in about ten minutes," he promised with a heavy sigh, but he was lying — I waited for half an hour and Mr. Mašek never showed up: it wasn't worth his trouble and, in the end, the whole Motor Rest and the Big Tuna weren't worth his trouble either. His towing business was booming, he happened to have a piece of a major truck route between Western Europe and the Middle East, because the fighting in the old Yugoslavia had rerouted all the cargo traffic his way, and he probably didn't bother to climb into his truck unless there was a Turkish rig or a German Mercedes broken down somewhere.

Once I realized Mr. Mašek wasn't coming after all, it took only a couple of minutes to get the car going: three young men from Ostrava gave me a push, starting my car the Czech way, the way Mašek had suggested.

I drove off from the billboard marveling at how utterly superfluous it was — Mr. Mašek had put it up because he figured this was what he was supposed to do. Businesses advertised, and he was aping what he thought businesses did, but his notion of customer service was a gold-digger's caricature of the concept: as far as Mr. Mašek could tell, businessmen skinned their customers and the commercial life was all gravy. He probably felt so rich he didn't think he needed anybody anymore — as a Czech idea of an Open Economy, it was perfect.

Yet, for every Mr. Mašek the country had someone like the Fed-Ex Man. He rang my bell one morning. He had come to pick up a package I was sending. "I'm not ready for you yet," I had to tell him, "so come on in, it'll only be a minute." In Czechoslovakia the floors got more consideration than the Immortal Soul — the Fed-Ex Man slipped off his shoes and tiptoed into our hallway in his socks.

WAR IN PRAGUE

When we arrived in Prague, Sonja could only understand a few phrases in Czech. Adam still had a smattering of the language, but with the vocabulary of a four-year-old: he went to potty, he had a Daddy and a Mommy — the Czech nine-year-olds were highly amused by his remarks and Adam quickly clammed up.

Both kids had the summer to pick up some of the language. In September, when the Czech public school down the hill from us opened, they were the only foreigners anyone could remember ever attending the place, but with a lot of after-hours help from us, they fought through their Sink-Or-Swim Crash-Course in Practical Czech.

One fall evening, Sonja was reading to me when I noticed she was scratching her head a lot — she would really dig her nails into her scalp too. Then I went to help Adam with his homework and saw that he couldn't keep his hands out of his hair, either. Immediately I began to feel crawly itchy twitchy tangs around my ears too — it turned out to be the sensation of the Invisible Hand of the Market working the post-Communist Czechoslovakia.

I never actually got to see a louse, but you couldn't miss their tell-tale nits — a hard white speck firmly attached halfway up a hair stem. They drove my wife to the verge of hysteria: "Oh, my God, this is so awful! Why did we come here?! This is so disgusting! Everything is so filthy here, so polluted, so unhealthy! What're we doing here?! How could we have brought children to this place?! I feel them crawling around my scalp too! I wanna go back home!"

The Czech lice were tough. They lived right through all the shampoos, conditioners, even the nasty domestic kerosene-based *Diffusil* — the only foolproof delousing remedy was to shave one's head, a measure my wife refused even to contemplate. But she declared an All-Out Chemical Manual Medicinal Anything-Goes Catch-As-Catch-Can War on Lice and, in a few days, we all managed to get rid of the critters while keeping our hair.

Afterward on the Metro, I'd watch my kids inch away from anyone who was scratching their head: Prague was proving to be as good an education for them as I'd hoped, yet suddenly you saw how full of lice the city was — on every block, you could spot a boy with a shaven head or a girl with closely cropped hair. What was going on? In my sixteen years in Czechoslovakia, over the course of my entire childhood, I'd only come across lice once, and it was a very big deal. In fact, in the sixties, there was a joke about a Soviet visitor of the country sneering: "You Czechs think you've got culture?! Ha, ha! I've yet to see a single delousing station in this country!"

Yet in the fall of 1992, the Prague newspapers were reporting a lice epidemic. Had nature evolved a strand of bionic lice under Communism? Was it all related to the devastated environment? Had everything in the country gone down, including the hygiene? And was this a matter of lingering Communist legacy or was it a post-Communist phenomenon? Wasn't it a symptom of Capitalist Poverty creeping in?

It was another grammar school teacher who finally gave me the score on the Great Lice Epidemic of the Early Nineties: "Well, the first thing our kids noticed about the lice was that if they had 'em, they got sent home from school. And they got to stay home till they were deloused, which always took a few days. So right away they figured out that lice were a little vacation from school: we caught them selling lice to each other. Back then, a louse ran you five crowns . . ."

A phone call cost a crown, a newspaper was about three crowns. You sold a louse and you could buy yourself a sticky glass of lemonade or some sweets — no wonder the louse market was soon going through the roof: "It was incredible," the teacher said, "before you knew it, a louse was going for twenty crowns! And my classroom was half-empty! A kid would come back lice-free and, that same day, he'd have them again and I'd have to send him back home . . . You couldn't teach anything." But in the end the market corrected itself. "It got so bad that we just stopped sending them home. Everybody had lice anyway, so what was the difference? So we just let them sit there and scratch their heads." The louse market crashed immediately. "The lice vanished so fast it was funny. In a couple of weeks, no one in my class was missing and no one was scratching their head, either."

And so Adam Smith had it right — the economy was all about incentive, and the Invisible Hand of the Market had a firm grip on Prague after all.

ZIPPER

As the Czechs rushed to catch up with the rest of the Use-and-Discard Global-Village Junk-Bond Western World, new businesses came and went in Prague at such a rate that you had to be careful whom you dealt with. Petr Sís, the Prague painter who moved to New York and became an illustrator of Wonderful Dreamy Surreal Tooth-of-Time-Gnawed Children's Books, dropped his top-of-the-line Nikon camera while visiting his people in the Lesser Quarter. He asked his younger brother to get it fixed for him — services in Prague cost a fraction of what they cost in New York. The brother took the busted Nikon into the nearest camera shop. He was given a receipt and told to come back in three weeks, but didn't get back to the shop till some five weeks later — the store wasn't there anymore. The door was locked, the empty shop window littered with scraps of paper.

The owners of the establishment had left no forwarding address. The younger Sís tracked down the man who owned the building, but didn't learn much from him. The guy said he had raised the camera store's rent and its owners loaded everything into a truck and took it away. They didn't tell him where they were going. There was no Better Business Bureau to call; the city government didn't keep any register of businesses; the police would only take a report and file it — Petr Sís never saw his Nikon again.

The massive changes in Prague disoriented people — the geography of neighborhoods was changing as fast as the maps of Eastern Europe: sitting on the Metro one day, I overheard a conversation between two teenage girls. One of them had a new pair of reflective wrap-around sunglasses.

"Oooh, cool specs!" said the other girl. "Where'd you get 'em?"

"You know that new drugstore down the street by me?" said her friend.

"Where the old video store was?"

"No, this place was a travel agency before."

"Oh, yeah! Wasn't it a pet shop too, at one time?"

"No, the pet shop was on the corner."

"Where that cleaner's is now?"

"No, the cleaner's used to be next door, where they had that pub later, you know? But this place was a travel agency for a while and now it's a drugstore . . ."

The rate of change in Prague reminded me of an eye-popping ride in a carnival contraption called the Zipper — you're strapped into a cabin which rotates around its point of suspension; the cabin hangs on an arm which also rotates vertically; the arm is a part of a gigantic Ferris wheel. The whole thing is made of creaking metal and it squeaks as it slowly sets in its three vertical motions and the calculus of the three centrifugal forces soon gives you some extraordinary sensations: one second you're hurling toward the ground as if you were going straight down in a fighter plane with the afterburners on full throttle, the next second everything freezes and you hang fifty feet above the stopped world and taste eternity — for a brief moment . . .

In Prague, it seemed at times that the whole country was strapped into the Zipper and the carny at its controls had just had him a little sip and was fighting to keep his eyes open.

BOOK
OF THE
DREAM
SELF

FIRST IMPRESSION

The Egyptian pyramids were nearly two thousand years old when the world's greatest tourist went to see them. They were already scarred with old Greek graffiti on the order of "Kilroy was here," but this tourist was Greek too and the witless inscriptions charmed him enough to get a mention in the ambitious book of history and travel he was writing — the time was the fifth century before Christ and the tourist's name was Herodotus.

Tourists were people who lived on first impressions and, in a strange place, it was often the familiar that made the biggest impact — like Herodotus, most tourists traveled to find a reflection of themselves in a faraway destination. And this was how we too entered Prague: reading the English-language weekly *Prague Post,* eyeballing all the required sights (blocked out by the natives a long time ago) and heading to the Charles Bridge every night.

The American Abroad in us reveled in the Postcard-In-The-Making Beauty of the bridge; the American Child dug the street performers that worked it. A few puppeteers ran through the same skits over and over again as if they had just punched in for a nine-to-five job, but there was also a brilliant mime drawing dead-on caricatures on the air, two fine ballerinas with a ghetto blaster risking their toes on the uneven, slippery cobblestones, drunken sword-swallowers and fire-eaters burning their tongues and throats, and, on a really good evening, the Last Chance, a wonderful quintet of Russian musicians. They played swinging parodies of rock 'n roll on a gigantic, stand-up balalaika and tiny chimes, a cello and a kid's pipe organ, strange pipes, accordions, and guitars, then launched into songs that transported you from the heart of the Deep Morning-Of-Your-Execution Russian Melancholy into the heart of the Deep Glass-Breaking Midnight-At-A-Wedding Russian Delirium.

You didn't see too many Czechs on the bridge, for the people of Prague were mostly ashamed of the carnival atmosphere, the flea-market vibes, and the bric-a-brac kitsch on sale there. "I hate to imagine what all these foreigners must think about us . . ." a young doctor spooked herself earnestly, "They've gotta think we're a bunch of gypsies here!"

The Czechs dreamed the dream of being Another Neat Clean Sterile Switzerland and kept away from the tourist-ridden spots, but it was on the Charles Bridge that we stopped being tourists and Prague became home to us — and I could pinpoint the very moment down to the second.

HARD-WORKING GUY

It was that odd moment when a thought no sooner crosses your mind than it becomes reality. Carrying Sonja on my shoulders, with Adam tagging along behind me, I was pushing through a knot of tourists on the stone bridge — they were humming "I can't get no/no satisfaction/no, no, no/ hey, hey, hey" with Ice, the Brazilian sing-along guitar player in grandma glasses — when I suddenly realized: I'm the perfect mark for a pickpocket right now — right then, I felt a light-fingered hand grope around my pocket.

I reached for my wallet which, thank God, was still there in the other pocket and, at the same time, I swung around — the guy on my heels was staring straight through me, his poker-faced lack of reaction to my abrupt turnaround a dead giveaway, so I started finger-pointing and yelling in English: "Pickpocket! This guy here is a pickpocket! Watch out everybody! This guy in the white shirt is a thief!"

With an amazing speed, the pickpocket backed away from me, slipping through the densely packed limbs as if he were a wet stick of soap. His face remained a mask and he never even looked at me, but I'd gotten a good look at him: he was a young gypsy in a blazing white shirt, not very big, not at all moved, quick, a weasel, gone long before his smell of cologne and starch drifted away.

The following night on our walk to the Charles Bridge, the kids raced ahead, forgetting their American prayer ("I hope somebody chooses me to do something in their act tonight . . .") and, sure enough, they quickly located the gypsy. He had on a fresh shirt and loitered around Ice's singing tourists again with two other men, both ethnic Czechs. I remembered their faces. They'd stepped between us and allowed him to melt away so quickly: they were his team.

That evening, our whole family marched right up to the thieves and proceeded to stare the pickpocket down — a moment later, the gypsy was overcome by the intoxicating beauty of the setting. He headed down the Baroque "Avenue of Saints," strolling as if he were staggered by the statuary: was he checking if Angelo Ripellino had got it right when he wrote that, in the works of the sculptor Matyáš Braun, "the stone dances"? Was he seeing "robes reminiscent of flooded rivers, waterfalls of lace, billowing coats" in the worn sandstone?

We stayed on his heels. The pickpocket walked faster. He made for the two-winged stairway descending to the man-made Isle of Kampa, ran down, and crossed the tree-lined square of the old potters' market. Did he cast those short glances over his shoulder to check if Bohumil Hrabal had gotten the view down when he reported that "seen from Kampa, the Charles Bridge looks like a long bathtub, through which the pedestrians slide on their butts as if on wheel gadgets; in the water below, Prague groans with broken ribs and, like baying hounds, one after the other, the arches of the bridge skip across the river?" Or was it the poetry of Jaroslav Seifert that rang in his ears? Was he imagining how the market had looked once, and seeing "the potters hang around their stands/tapping on the pitchers/they have flowers in their hands?"

The gypsy knew the terrain as well as the great poets of Prague. He slipped through a narrow passage and vanished into the flood-prone island — having no church and no basements, Kampa was said to be crawling with phantoms, ghosts, unreleased souls, aborted spirits, and spectral misfits.

But after that summer evening, we started coming to the Charles Bridge to watch the pickpocket ply his trade, watch the pushers of artsy souvenirs jockey for the spots in the lee of the saints on the windy bridge, watch the musicians push out the perimeters of their sound, watch all those things we hadn't noticed before — and Prague became home to us, because home was the place where the first impressions had lost their punch, where you saw through the studied gesture to the true self, where you perceived the deeper realities of life.

DREAM SELF

Like Venice, Granada, or Paris, Prague was fast becoming a place you couldn't imagine without the tourists — they were clogging up the Old Town and the Lesser Quarter, trudging behind the raised umbrellas of their guides, snapping the same pictures of the same sights over and over again, woven now into the fabric of the city even while they rarely rubbed up against its authentic life. (They inhabited their standard International Tourist Buffer which enclosed all the mass-travel destinations: they were waited and preyed on by tourist hustlers, who mauled their languages, affected their mannerisms, and emptied their wallets by pushing a few cultural buttons.)

Where there were tourists, there were also the expatriates: by some estimates, Prague was home to as many as twenty thousand Americans. The number was endlessly disputed and iffy, but Prague *did* have a couple of English-language weeklies as well as a literary journal, an American laundromat, pizzerias, American nightclubs, theater groups, and sports bars. The expatriates didn't rush around with checklists of not-to-be-missed sights, didn't chase the traditional dish or the typical handicrafts, or blow vacation budgets. They didn't live by first impressions and didn't look for a reflection of themselves in Prague — the expatriates often kept busy nurturing their dream selves.

When the young New York writer Camille Sweeney examined the expatriate scene, she found that many Americans had come for a sort of a Midlife Pause: they were often just out of college and hadn't yet figured out what to do with themselves. Some were merely taking a break from the Stressful Rat-Race Suit-And-A-Tie American Life, some came for the Ride on the Pony of Post-Communism, others for the romance of being Americans abroad, still others "to find themselves."

These expatriates didn't try to fit into Prague, for they often hadn't fit in at home, either — Prague was merely a place where you could wear your dream self cheaply. It was a city where, if you thought you probably, maybe, quite possibly, were a writer, you could try the role on for size — drink great beer all night and sleep all day, read a little Kafka, work on a poem, enjoy the fetal comfort of being surrounded by a wall of impenetrable language, take streetcars, get laid without the fear of AIDS, borrow a little money from friends, crash at someone's pad, teach a little English, sneer at soccer while talking up baseball, write a journal, form a rock band, eyeball the strange Slavic proletariat, hang out with the hip locals, read a little Hemingway on being an expatriate in Paris, float in monumental cholesterol, pig out in the local pubs and feel guilty or bad-boy heroic about it, glance at the sights through a bar window, read a little Gertrude Stein, write long letters, talk shop with other literati, smoke to your heart's content, let your body rot and never hear a word about it, get a Czech girlfriend who would let you lie on a sofa and read a book while she mopped the floor, and become a drinker with a writing problem.

One night, I went to case an American poetry reading, a benefit for the Prague English-language literary journal, called *Yazzyk*. It took place in a basement of the massive *Ženské Domovy* dormitory building in *Smíchov* and the place was packed — there were several hundred mostly American Young Lit-Type Expats, spilling from the chairs onto a wide staircase and drinking good beer out of waxy paper cups.

Youthful poets and writers stepped up to a microphone and shared their works in progress, but this was no Chicago-style Poetry Slam: there was little attempt to entertain the audience or to connect with it — these young men and women mostly droned on and on with their Interminable Self-Involved Angst-Ridden Punky Confessional Poems and Precious Hermetic Stories while a respectful hush reigned in the room, for everyone had come here to celebrate the High Mass of the Religion of Literature. (And this particular mass was celebrated in Latin too, which became clear when the silence stretched on even while a few poems were read in Czech, a language that very few people in the room understood.)

It slowly dawned on me that I'd strayed into the *Yazzyk* zone, and that I should have been prepared for this Massive Stroking of the Collective Dream Self, for it had all been right there in the name of the literary magazine: "*Yazzyk*" was a Prague-American expatriate neologism that said nothing in English and nothing in Czech. As an English phonetic transcription of the Czech word *jazyk* ("tongue" or "language"), the word had no meaning at all in English, while the Czechs couldn't decipher the bizarre spelling, either — "*Yazzyk*" was an in-joke, a password for the initiated, the Perfect Secret Cabalistic Misfit Term for the Young American Priests of the Religion of the Incomprehensible Literature.

But why would this strange creed appeal to anyone? Why would an artist want to shut himself or herself off into a secret language? Didn't writers reflect and explain the world? Didn't they name things? And why would anyone ever go to such lengths in order not to fit?

Maybe it was because the insiders had a quick way of deflating the dream self as they asked their dumb, boorish, insensitive questions: Made any money at it? What odds would a bookie give you? What's the contingency plan here? And then what? And then what? And then?

And so, when you had a dream self to maintain, wasn't it easier not to fit in anywhere at all?

FOREIGN CORRESPONDENT

Mike Persson was a young expatriate who didn't need a dream self. When I met the up-and-coming photographer in Prague, he had bagged his first cover of *Newsweek*. A short, wiry wolverine of a man with long blond hair in a ponytail, he could have fit in anywhere in the world: in Prague, he learned enough Czech to carry a conversation in a bar and keep all the barflies in stitches — he was quick-witted, rude in a sensitive way, funny and game for anything, had a little boy's curiosity and excitability, and kept spinning off entertaining streams of Baroque obscenities. You hardly even noticed that, all the while, he was working his camera too.

Persson was genuinely a citizen of the world: born to a Swedish blond in Malmö, Sweden, he never knew his Croatian father — "me old man was in the importing business in Malmö, but he fucked off before I was born . . . He was importing heroin and he had to make himself scarce in a hurry one day . . ." The old man repaired to Dubrovnik only to be shot there — "I don't think it happened while he was stealing towels from a hotel, either" — so Persson had never met him.

When he was twelve, Persson's mother married a British business-man, and he came of age in London, where he had picked up Thai kick-boxing and a vigorous working-class accent. The crowd he ran with stole cars and torched them for kicks — "Jags burn the best, *mano* . . . They're easy to break into, fun to light up, a real pyro-maniac's dream . . . You don't wanna torch a Porsche, too bloody bor-ing . . . No bang and rather a job."

When Persson was released from the reformatory, his stepfather took the family to California for a couple of years, but Persson didn't care for America. He always knew he was going to be a photographer and had the drive of an illegitimate kid who wanted to show the whole world — he returned to London and became a gofer to a famous photographer in London, then quickly his first assistant, and then, when he had learned everything there was to learn there, he struck out on his own. As a freelancer, he made straight for where the most dramatic images were coming from.

During the Iraqi war, he "ran with the media pack" in Kurdistan, taking advantage of the fact that he could "make himself small enough to get to the front of the pack and not get into anybody's way," and learning the finer points of being a foreign correspondent, such as when to return a rented car riddled with bullet holes and when to ditch it to everyone's relief, but wolverines hunt alone: "I didn't care for it . . . You're sitting in a bar, somebody comes up with a scoop, everybody jumps into a car, then it's the bloody Indy 500 to get there, and then you rock 'n roll elbowing fifty other pack rats for the angle of the shot . . ."

And so Persson relocated to Yugoslavia and talked his way into the graces of Arkan the Serbian war criminal. "Arkan had run the soccer rowdies of the Red Star of Belgrade before the war. Then he set up his Tigers" — the *Légion Etrangère* of Serbia — "he pulled them up from all the shitholes of society. He had soccer hooligans, skins, jail birds, macho nuts, soldiers of fortune, but they were all ready to drop on a hand grenade for him, even though he was a ruthless disciplinarian . . ."

Persson stuck with the Tigers as they advanced into the Krajina region which the Serbs were just wrestling away from Croatia. "Arkan's boys killed civilians all the time . . . They'd take a village and go and do what they called 'purging by blood.' They'd walk through and shoot everything that moved: kids, old people, cows, pigs, dogs, roosters . . . The bestiality was incredible . . ." It was understood that Persson was not to take pictures of "blood purging," or the executions of civilians, but he managed to document some of these killings on the sly: "I was with the Tigers when they broke the siege of Vukovar," where the Croatian defenders had held out for several weeks even after the city had been completely leveled. "The Tigers got so carried away they became drunk with blood lust and careless . . ."

You wondered how Persson had been able to take it. Was it as a wolverine? Or as the true, cynical foreign correspondent? The ambitious kid? He was half-Croatian by blood: did that make it worse? Or given his rogue old man, did that in fact make it easier?

Purely from the practical point of view, the father was a liability: "I was teetering on the edge all the time I was with the Tigers anyway, and if Arkan had found out that me Pops was a Croatian, I woulda been a dead Persson before I coulda told him I ain't never had a bloody occasion to call the old boy Daddy . . ."

The images that Persson brought back from the Balkans, however, kicked you right in the gut, even while their composition made you think of Delacroix — you were there while three handsome Serbian soldiers fired a rocket-propelled hand grenade out of the safety of a swirl of terrified civilians. These warriors had tuned out the human cries a long time ago, but still recoiled from the weapon's bang. They wore golden watches and starched uniforms, looking trim, vain, and parade-ground handsome, as if their war was a fancy blood sport with a dress code.

Another photograph froze a moment in a landscape of lush, green hills: an open-bay construction truck had backed up to the spot where it was about to dump its cargo. You saw the cargo bay from behind, saw the truck driver hanging out his door and staring back as he lifted the bay, a professional taking pride in his job. His load was tilted high now, but hadn't set in motion yet — it hung suspended in that precarious moment just before jerking into a slow slide and tumbling into the tall green grass, a pile of dead limbs intertwined with wheelbarrows and shovels, for this was how the Muslims and the Croats exchanged their dead in Bosnia Hercegovina: the civilians twisted in their bloody T-shirts and skirts and flipflops, and woven together into a quantum of death which their relatives would have to sort out and pry apart from construction tools, before cutting the torn clothing off the bodies, before washing off the caked blood, before brushing the fly eggs off the purple, smelly wounds of their dear mothers and fathers and wives and husbands and daughters and sons — all the while boiling with mad fury.

DINNER FROM HELL

While in the Balkans, some ten hours away by car, people were dying of starvation, the expatriates, the tourists, and the returned émigrés were introducing Prague to the art of fine dining — one summer night in 1992, I tagged along with a bunch of VIPs from the Czech film industry to wine and dine an elderly Hollywood producer and found myself in a restaurant that fancied itself one of the Top Total Dining Experiences in the city.

The Parnassus offered a to-die-for view of the Vltava River, the Charles Bridge, and Hradčany Castle, and it also happened to be run by a Boston-based corporation, which had leased the building for the next 99 years. I thought it was a good thing that American corporations were becoming a presence in Prague, figuring they would pull up the Czech business standards by forcing the natives to compete with their Efficient Rational Service-Oriented Quality-Controlled Invisible-Hand-Sculpted Operations.

Entering the Parnassus on a hot night, I wished the Bostonians had thought a little more American and put in air-conditioning: the wood-paneled dining room had the temperature of a girl-mud-wrestling bar in Florida. We were shown to a corner table, far from the spectacular views which we had booked, and served a wineglass of beer, warm enough to bathe a sneezing baby in.

"What do you want *me* to do?" the head waiter was unbowed, "our electrical system is antiquated and it's overwhelmed."

Since we had to drink something warm, we ordered a couple of bottles of red wine. The waitress was a sweet young thing, but she knocked over the first bottle while uncorking the second one. The falling bottle broke our water pitcher and bled burgundy all over the soaked table cloth. There followed airline food in airline portions — this was clearly the Dinner from Hell, even before Eva Ondříčková, the Vessel of the Last Drops of Hussite Blood in the Country, focused on the plate of the American visitor: "That's no duck," she said, "That thing right there is chicken."

This was not an accusation to be brought lightly in a restaurant where the bill for eight people would come out to more than a hundred hard-cover books, so we all carefully examined the meat — yes, it did look white and remarkably chicken-like, and yes, it did taste dry and remarkably chicken-like too.

The manager was an East Indian who could only smile, say, "I sorry I not speaking Czech," and retreat, so I stopped him and explained what our problem seemed to be in English.

The manager's smile hardened. "Dat absolutely is duck," he pointed at the white meat. His pundit's air of authority reminded me of an Indian doctor who, by way of diagnosis, had informed a friend with severe abdominal pains that "da Stomach is da Temple of Mystery."

"I've been cooking duck all my life," Eva Ondříčková raised her voice in reply. "And I've been cooking chicken all my life. This isn't duck. It's too white, it's too dry, and the cut is too thick! This is chicken!"

I translated her words in the same tone of voice. The background hum of conversations faded out.

"Well, all right," the Indian conceded, "but dat is not chicken!" He made a long pause. He was clearly thinking on his feet. What precious bird was he going to come up with? Partridge? Nightingale? Ostrich? Toucan? Macaw? The bald eagle? Or something truly endangered? The last California condor? He took a deep breath and informed us solemnly: "Dat is turkey."

I'd been a corpo dynamo in Chicago for ten years — I didn't know what had ever possessed me to think that an American corporation would lead the process of change in Czechoslovakia when it could just as profitably sink to the prevailing standards: the American-run Parnassus fit into Prague's Caricature of the Tourist Industry like a fat Boston butt on a Baroque chamber pot.

BOOK
OF
MANNERS

OLD SCHOOLMATE IN A NEW BMW

As creakily as the Invisible Hand had set the wheel of the Czech economy spinning, it quickly upset the order of Prague's society. Under Communism, the Beautiful People of Czechoslovakia had included aging Communist party playboys like the prime minister, Štrougal, prominent sportsmen, film stars, pop singers, and money changers, but the lukewarm revolution had melted this class away like the snows of yesteryear. Also gone was the flip side of the Beautiful World, the underground ghetto of dissidents — those who'd had a corner on real class, because they weren't afraid to live in truth and take the consequences.

In the Prague of the early nineties, speculators, real-estate sharpies, advertising gurus, porno-pushers, and ministers with blatant conflicts of interest were making fortunes, and no one bothered to stake out the moral high ground. The pecking orders pitched and yawed so erratically that people who paid attention to such things were stressed out.

"I have no idea where I fit anymore," the fine jazz singer Irena Budweiserová told me, "and it just drives me crazy. I'll think I'm doing great and then I see an old schoolmate in a new BMW and I realize I'm falling behind and I'll never catch up."

Budweiserová's remark made me wonder: what benchmarks did you use in Prague to figure out your social standing? How did you place yourself in this world? And were there any enduring structures in Prague society? What institutions have survived the quick succession of monarchy, democracy, fascism, communism, and post-communism over the past eighty years?

ABOVE THE KNEE

In Chicago, Butthole Surfers, Dead Kennedys, and slam dancing were footnotes in history and the Cunt Coloring Book sold briskly in lesbian bookstores. In Prague, teenagers flocked to ballroom dance lessons where they learned to mazurka, waltz, always to stroll to the left of the lady, and never to kiss a gloved hand — the longest-lasting society institution in Prague was the *Taneční*, a network of Ballroom Dance and Etiquette Lessons with a branch in every small town. This Czech tradition had started in high society under the Habsburg monarchy, seeped into the lower classes, spreading throughout the country, and went on to thrive under all the governments that followed.

It was Mike Persson who had alerted me to the *Taneční:* "You just have to come and see this," he told me one day, "it's un-fucking-believable."

He was shooting a photo-essay on Prague's most popular dance lessons and he took me along to the Marble Hall of Lucerna Palace on Wenceslas Square. There was a large parquet floor, a small stage, a wall of gilded mirrors, an ambulatory with marble columns — and, most monumentally, Mrs. Karasová.

A dynamo of a perfect lady in whose plump body beat the heart of a boot camp sergeant, Mrs. Karasová had been running the Lucerna *Taneční* for over twenty years. She was in her early fifties now, elegant in a bottle-green evening gown set off by a simple pearl necklace, and impeccably coiffed and manicured. She proudly gave me a tour of her work place.

"This ballroom has been designed specifically for dance classes," she pointed out the huge crystal chandeliers, the wine-colored velvet curtains, and the matching Biedermeier chairs. "I went to my own *Taneční* here. I took the same dance lessons as our Mr. President." She was talking about Václav Havel — Prague *was* a small world. "Of course back then, they made money with thirty-five students in a class. Nowadays, we can barely stay even with a hundred and sixty . . ."

Mrs. Karasová taught fourteen two-hour classes a week and still couldn't fully meet the demand: "The night before we start signing people up, we've got parents with sleeping bags camping outside our office door — and that's only the girls' Moms and Dads, mind you! The boys take care of themselves . . ."

The girls were encouraged to bring a *garde dame* to the lessons — "it's the parents who hold the purse strings and they want to get something out of this whole thing too, even though our mothers go ballistic when they see their daughters sit out a dance." Not to worry, because, in Mrs. Karasová's world, there was a solution for every problem: "So we assign about ten more boys than girls to each class. Our boys are glad to get off the dance floor for a spell . . ."

On that cold November night, the polka with the full turn on the eighth step was taught. Mrs. Karasová and her Biedermeier husband, wide of belly, nimble of foot ("he was a weight lifter, you see, but now he's on Herbalife . . . Lost eight kilos already, but it's making him pretty mean") demonstrated the complicated steps, spinning lightly around the dull parquet floor.

Watching the fluid grace of the elderly, overweight couple, the gawky students giggled nervously. The boys stood lined up on one side of the room, wearing bow ties and white gloves. The girls faced them across the dance floor. They wore elbow-length gloves and evening dresses that ranged in style from cool Grace-Kelly elegance to a shocking-pink fluffy figure-skating-skirted number with fingerless gloves that a Marengo hooker would die for. The *gardes dames* fidgeted on the ornate chairs behind their daughters, craning their necks to peer around their hips.

Mrs. Karasová lucidly broke down the steps of the polka, then climbed the stage and issued a calm order: "Gentlemen, claim your partners!"

The boys took off across the dance floor, a Stampeding Hormone Herd, dashing madly for the prettiest girls, pushing and elbowing each other. After a brief skirmish, the most desirable partners were grabbed and there came a desperate scrambling for alternatives.

Finally, half a dozen boys who hadn't gotten any girl at all strolled back under the ambulatory, feigning relief. (They would in fact get to take over the girls of their choice in a few minutes, because the lesson was craftily organized on the principle of a constant switching of partners.)

"You there, the tall miss in the pink dress . . ." Mrs. Karasová went to work: "Yes, you . . . You who came in late, shall we get rid of the chewing gum? We can suck our thumbs if we have an inexorable oral compulsion . . ." The put-downs were part of the twisted entertainment. "Now the young lady in the yellow skirt down here, shall we stop hanging on our partner as if he were a coat hanger? Extend your arm . . ."

At last, the three-man band on the stage struck up the polka as slow as it would go and, struggling with the complicated steps, it was everyone against their own feet and everyone else's feet.

"Okay, ladies and gentlemen! Enough torture! On to the *grande promenade!*" Mrs. Karasová finally sent her pimply Ghosts of the Habsburg High Society to march under the ambulatory, "we've made it without any fractures today which I find highly satisfying." A titter of giggles. "Don't guffaw, please! I had three falls in Wednesday's class! Now gentlemen, if your lady falls down on the floor, you pick her up! Don't you dare run away!" A burst of laughter. "Now ladies, if your partner falls down, you leave him there! Don't you pick him up!" A howl of laughter. "The most you can do for him is to stand over him like a policeman, so that the other dancers don't trample him."

And so, with celestial authority, the Victorian double-standards began to tumble into the post-feminist world. Mrs. Karasová's rules of etiquette prescribed that, when a lady greeted a lady, the whole encounter turned entirely on their respective social ranking: "If you work for a younger woman, you've absolutely got to greet her first! I don't care if you're sixty and she's only twenty!"

The dance mistress had told me earlier that she was thinking about starting her own *Taneční* next year, so after the lesson, I asked her if she'd still be using the same Victorian guide of manners as now — this booklet advised her students that "the crossing of legs by the ladies is a rather problematic thing. The legs should not really be crossed above the knee."

"Oh, yes. Oh, absolutely, we'll use that guide!" Mrs. Karasová told me with her vintage Take-No-Prisoners Damn-the-Torpedoes confidence.

Just how current were these rules?

"Our rules of etiquette have *never* been updated, not since the Dance Lessons here started, never, not a line!"

Mrs. Karasová was talking about a half-century of time, yet she didn't see any reason to change a thing in her profession: she was a beacon in the lives of her students — the Perfect Matriarch, powerful in her confidence in herself in all situations, never at a loss for words, always ready with a solution. And these days, her old students were forever turning up with babies at Mrs. Karasová's door, cute little tykes who wouldn't have been born if it weren't for her, because their parents had met in her *Taneční* ("it gets a little awkward sometimes because I don't always remember them — there've been tens of thousands of youths and, at that age, very few of them had as yet developed distinct character"), her younger students were sometimes calling on her in the wee hours of the morning, crying ("sometimes I wish I was a psychologist — the tears are usually a good sign though, I know *that*"), and so many of the lives she had touched seemed to be in need of her Big Shoulder to Lean On ("I do what I can").

And the rewards?

"I'll tell you about a really satisfying moment . . . There was a boy in my *Taneční* who'd had polio. He walked with a cane. He was a brave kid — always hung the cane in the coatcheck and did his best on the dance floor. But we have a ladies' choice night, and I thought, what if he just has to sit there all night?! My God, he could be devastated . . . Well, I called his parents and they kept him home from a lesson, so that I could talk to the other kids openly. And boy, did I talk to them! I went straight for their gut, I said: Now you picture yourselves in his place! Just for one minute, you just limp to that coatcheck in your mind right now and you ask for that cane and you grip it tight and you lean on it and you limp out of that door! Just think of how that feels! And now think about something else too: I'd hate to see it happen, but you just never know, What if you get run over by a streetcar on the way home tonight? What if one day you wind up in a wheelchair yourselves?"

One week later, the boy with the polio danced all night. And the most beautiful girl in the class had asked him for the first dance — "she was truly exquisite, she's a model now . . . You should have seen the expression on his face. He's still thinking back on it, that I'm sure of. I know people who've lived off much less for the rest of their lives."

GARDES DAMES

In 1969, in the Provincial Town of Thirty Thousand Souls, without pausing to think why, I'd put down one hundred and fifty crowns as my deposit for that fall's course of the *Taneční*. I was sixteen and all my buddies were buying tuxedos and bow ties — it just happened to be something that everybody did. (In their time, my parents too had clumsily spun around the same squeaky floor of that same ballroom to the loud counting of a dance teacher.) But that summer, we left the country, so I never learned the polka with the turn on the eighth step which was part of the discontent of civilization in the Provincial Town — belatedly, in the Marble Room of the Lucerna building in Prague, it all caught up with me.

They were all there: the tall thoughtful girl, the vain blond, the tomboy with a prison haircut, the fifteen-year-old matron, the sexy kitten, the fat girl in a radical miniskirt, the shy, bright observer with glasses and nails bitten to the quick . . . They strolled past the gilded mirrors on the arm of the boy who forgot his white gloves, and kept exploding in ripples of embarrassed laughter — the boy who could have been me, because all the boys I remembered were there too: the born dancer, the candidate for stomach ulcers, the brooding winner, the future engineer concentrating grimly and counting the turns out loud . . .

Yes, this was exactly how it must have been twenty-three years earlier, in that *Taneční* I'd paid for and missed — the losers pairing up with each other; those who had got the hang of it being stepped on by the "sauerkraut stompers"; the couples who were able to dance and talk spinning around the couples who were dying for something halfway witty to say and coming up empty; the narcissists constantly checking the mirror; the embraceable ghosts . . .

In Lucerna's Marble Room, though, I saw things I would never have noticed back in Kolín: I saw how tired the *garde dames* were, saw how wearily they reclined on the burgundy velvet of the balding upholstery, saw how their plump calves sagged beside the swan-neck legs of the Beidermeier chairs, saw the ubiquitous shopping bags shoved under them like strange eggs, saw how warily they eyeballed their daughters, saw the maternal gaze that was too loving beam on a girl who could do no wrong, saw the sour smile trained on a fine dancer who could never make it good enough, saw the dull regard of parental resignation, saw the eyes that took in only the swirls of pretty colors on the dance floor — the mothers would have been the enemy back in the Provincial Town, but they were my generation now and I had a daughter too and knew how feeble the enemy was, knew how little power it had, how worried about hormones it was, knew how weary it felt, and it shocked me, for I suddenly realized I'd somehow sleepwalked right across the front and wound up on the far side now, with nothing but pity for the poor enemy.

SUNDAY AFTERNOON

The Czech ears were still ringing with Communist propaganda and lies, and the Victorian rules of etiquette taught at the *Taneční* seemed only another Blast from the Double-Speak Past — the majority of Prague's citizens had gone through the *Taneční*, yet little in their everyday behavior bore the mark of Victorian grace: Prague was a city where, on a sunny Sunday afternoon, you could come close to having your bones crushed in a stampede of silent-majority types, and your children could get pissed on, and you were expected to think nothing of it.

It was a bright fall Sunday when I took the kids to a soccer game. *Sparta Praha* was playing *Bobby Brno* at its stadium in the *Letná* neighborhood. My own father had been a fanatical Sparta fan, and I had old memories of the place, but now the stadium was notorious for the "flag-bearers" — the skinheads and the soccer rowdies rampaging in its standing-room sections — and I was resolved to get some safe seats on the main tier.

I circled the entire looming structure, but found only a single window with sitting-room tickets. It peeked out of a massive cement wall right under the stadium's second tier. The concrete overhang, supported by thick steel pylons, opened onto *Letná* Avenue in the back, but the low, dark space under it had the feel of an underground garage. When I got there, a throng of fans was funneling to the ticket window, several hundred men with clocks ticking down to game-time in their heads, but there were no barriers, no ropes, no saw-horses, no security guards to control their impatience. And then the game started — you heard the fans oooohing and aaaaahing and groaning above you and sensed the excitement spilling from the stadium into the crowd — suddenly, the chaotic ticket line broke and everyone made a push for the window.

I grabbed Adam and Sonja before they got trampled, hustled them back to the edge of *Letná* Avenue, and left them near a mounted policeman: "You guys stay right here! I'll be back here with the tickets, but it might take a while, so don't move! Okay?!"

They nodded solemnly, and I plunged back into the Elbow-Swinging Tooth-Gritting Every-Grimly-Silent-Man-For-Himself Free-For-All. Leading with my shoulder, burrowing into the packed bodies sideways, I fought my way toward the window. I saw nothing before me but the backs of heads and shoulders, packed into a tight knot of pressing fans, when suddenly a hysterical face popped up in front of me — I was standing chest to chest with a balding young man who looked trapped and was in a frenzy about it. His eyes were bulging out, he was jerking his body every which way; finally, he started screaming: "Let me out! Let me out! Let me out, damn it!" He was staring right into my eyes.

"Take it easy, will you . . . I'd like to, believe me . . ."

"Let me out! Let me go! Out! Out!"

"Come on, man, what do you want me to do?"

"Let me outta here! Let me out! Let me out!"

He was practically foaming at the mouth now, spraying my face with his saliva, and I couldn't back out, couldn't get any leverage from my feet at all, couldn't get out of his way for the life of me. I couldn't even wipe off his spittle, because I needed both my arms to breathe — people were pressing into my back, harder and harder, squeezing the breath out of me, compressing my lungs: to inhale now, I had to wedge my arms into the guy and dig a little space for my chest out of him before I could finally suck in a snort of oxygen.

"Out! Out! Ooooooouuuuuut! Oooooooooooooooo!" he no longer articulated words, he was just ululating and spitting all over me.

It was an incredibly ridiculous moment — we were compressed into a tiny area inside a huge, empty space, a pretzeled pack of frenzied humanity in the corner of a concrete fortress which opened on a wide, cobbled avenue, with a huge parking lot beyond. I could turn my head and see Adam and Sonja dutifully standing some thirty yards away, see the mounted policeman right behind them, see a straggler hurry past us as if he didn't hear the ranting screams of the madman in my face, but my arms were pinned to my chest now, my ribs and shoulders were straining to hold back the bone-crushing pressure of feverish fans, I was wondering when something would give and I thought about the Iranian girl in the suitcase.

ELEPHANTS

Many years before, back in the days when Iranians still had money, I'd read a story of a pair of Iranian lovers in a newspaper. The young man lived in Los Angeles and had a green card, but his fiancée was having problems entering the country. They badly wanted to be together and, finally, came up with a simple plan to do it — he would just fly her from Paris into Los Angeles in a suitcase.

She was a small woman and they bought a huge, sturdy suitcase and thought everything would be okay. Did they test it out in Paris? Did she try zipping herself up in the thing for a couple of hours? Did he buy her a watch with a phosphorescent dial? Did he lug the suitcase to the elevator and ride up and down the building with her? Or was this something that you preferred not to think about? Did she figure she might never go through with the plan if she tried it? Was this something you just plunged into?

She clearly wasn't claustrophobic, because when the time came, she climbed into the suitcase. He zipped her up, hauled her to the airline counter, tied an address tag on the handle. Did he whisper to the suitcase? Did she whisper back? What were the last things they said? Some nervous last-minute smuggling instructions? Some words of tenderness? Was she beginning to feel any apprehension? Did she just suck it up? Did she share her dread with him? Did he answer? Did he say he was absolutely sure, just knew it, that she'd be fine? Did he tell her she was famous for underestimating her abilities? Or did he just hiss some terse good-byes to the suitcase as if he hadn't heard her?

He checked her in. The big suitcase was entered in the computer, weighed, and heaved on a conveyor belt. It brushed back the curtain of rubber strips behind the counter and disappeared.

Many hours later, in Los Angeles, the suitcase was found on a luggage carousel, the last piece of the Paris flight baggage still left there, unclaimed, going around and around and around — it was by imagining what had gone on inside that suitcase that I learned I could tap into the feeling of claustrophobia, that somehow the emotion was inside me, too: just think about being curled up in there, crammed into the fetal position, in pitch-black darkness in the City of Light, in the stale air, your hands gripping your ankles, your face on your knees, think of the beads of sweat tickling you everywhere, think of being compressed from all sides, think about having no control over what happened to you, think about how loud your heart would be beating . . .

Was she able to bear this horror by telling herself she could still put a stop to everything? She could always scream at the baggage handlers and get out any time she'd had enough, couldn't she? Or did she just block it all out? Was she resolved to endure anything and everything? Defeat fear, thrash all instinct, conquer biology for love?

She was carried by conveyor belt: think of the grinding below her, the gasping sensation of being lifted and swung, of flying through the air and landing painfully — did she wind up on her side? Upside down? The blood rushing into her head? Think of the sudden sense of an open space around her as she was wheeled across the runways to the plane. Was it raining? Did the rain drops give the huge, flat landscape around her a startling plasticity? Did the luggage cart pass any taxiing planes? Did it shake with the roar of their engines? Wasn't she scared then?

There followed the bobbing of a forklift, the sensation of going up, maybe one last chance to stop everything and get out — why didn't she? Why didn't she start screaming? Did she still believe? Was she that strong? Could love make you do anything at all?

She was dumped on the pile of luggage inside the belly of the plane, she surrendered to her fate completely. Now no one could hear anymore, now she could never get out, now she was luggage — think of the vibration as the jet engines cut on, robbing her of her voice, imagine the pounding she took as the other bags, boxes, suitcases, backpacks, packages started coming down on her, the terrible beating, the crushing weight taking her breath away, imagine being squeezed tighter and tighter, can't push back, can't move a finger anymore, not even an eyelid, and finally not even the tongue in her head, think of an elephant rolling over you, think the staggering pressure in the dark, your mouth a vertical, in the tiny black cavity, the jet engines roaring, knowing now this was your coffin, was she a virgin, think another elephant on top of the first one, fornicating, crushing your bones, the pain like a flame everywhere around you, sucking for air, the pain a fire inside you, your rib cage caving in, in the clouds, in the suitcase, the clouds like rocks and dirt on your coffin lid, buried alive, a bride forever, his forever.

He was only a few yards away, did he sense anything? How could he not? Did he glimpse the suitcase being loaded into the belly of the plane? Did he watch the rest of the luggage go in? Did it occur to him that they'd checked in too early? Did he realize something was wrong? Did he have a change of heart? Did he break into sweat? Did he pray? Did he think of her the whole flight?

Maybe he hadn't seen anything, maybe he thought everything was fine. Maybe he kicked his shoes off and ordered a drink. Did his mind drift to other pretty women on the flight? There were always pretty women flying into Los Angeles, did he look at them and think: you're too tall, you'd never fit into a suitcase; you're too stuck up, you'd never love anyone madly enough to get into a suitcase for him? Did looking at the pretty women on the plane make him proud of his fiancée? Did he love her more? Did he doze off?

At last the plane landed. They were in California together. Did he run through the snaking hallways? Did he rush through the immigration check-point? Did he try to play it cool? Did he figure that being in that suitcase five or ten minutes longer was no big deal? And what was their plan for getting through customs anyway? The suitcase was brought all the way from the plane to the luggage carousel, so they hadn't paid off anyone from the airline to stash it away in some hallway: what had they intended to do? Did he plan on simply throwing a coat over the suitcase behind some counter, unzipping it and letting her out? Did she imagine she'd just jump up and walk away after twelve hours in the suitcase? Were they going to leave the empty suitcase there? What had been going on in their heads?

The baggage handlers rushed to get the luggage out in Los Angeles. They hustled the stuff to the airport hall, they threw it on the carousel. Were they cursing the size on some of them big-ass ol' suitcases? The suitcase showed no sign of damage, no blood had leaked out, her body was stiff and cold now, her blood had clotted, nothing stained the carousel. The big suitcase kept going around and around till they shut off the conveyor belt.

How did he find out? Did he just look at the suitcase and know? Did he lift her up, did he feel the dead weight? Did he talk to her? Did he unzip the suitcase at all? He walked away. He staggered out into the hot California sun. He kept walking. The parched land, the oil derricks, the glare. He crossed some freeway. Was he cursed by the drivers? Damn fool, idiot, what a jerk, whattaya, nuts? Did he laugh? He had zipped her up, had tied the address tag on, had heaved her on the conveyor belt — there were no curses damning enough, no words adequate to what he had done. He wandered down the shoulder of a California freeway, slapped by the airwaves of the passing traffic, as regular as the surf not far off. In the city of cars, his home, the hum of engines, the roar of trucks, the dead weight of that suitcase, still going around the carousel. He waited for a big truck, its roar gaining on him, it was the sonic boom of a jet, not as loud as his heart, waited till it was almost level with him, waited, waited, now, he dove, he was with her.

PLANET ON A SUNDAY AFTERNOON

It was funny how, even in a compressed crowd where you had trouble breathing, you could still get away from a crazed stranger: somehow I managed to slither away from the guy. The pressure had eased slightly too, and with everyone else trying to get away from him, the poor guy was finally able to spit and holler his way out of the mob.

I had no control over my locomotion at all now, but the sluggish stream in the center of the mass of fans carried me straight to the ticket window — there, in his tiny fortress behind the thick glass, the Sparta ticket seller just sat and peered ahead impassively. He had nothing to do, because it took forever for someone to fight his way through to him. Didn't he realize what was going on right in front of his nose? Didn't he know he could save bones from being crushed simply by closing his window? Why didn't he just pull down the curtain? Didn't he care what happened?

He eyeballed me in a very detached way — clearly, thinking wasn't on this man's job description. I dropped my crumpled hundred-crown bill into his tray, slapped my palms on the thick glass of his window, and pushed back with all my strength just so the men wouldn't squash me against the wall. The ticket man didn't say anything. He took his sweet time peeling three tickets off the pink sheet in his gray booklet. He slipped them into the tray, shot me one last scientist glance, and was ready to serve the next customer.

I found the kids by a different pylon, deeper inside the overhang. They had moved only some ten yards, but I'd wanted them to stay close to the mounted policeman. "Listen, you guys! Next time when I tell you to stay somewhere and not move, I don't want you to move on me, all right?"

"Well, they were spilling beer on us from up there, Dad . . ." reported Adam.

"Oh . . . All right, then what you did was smart," I said, because I did leave them right under a walkway in the stands, but I didn't realize that Adam was being the diplomat he usually was.

"Some of 'em were peeing down too, Dad," Sonja the True Heart of the Family gave me the whole scoop on what could come to pass on a sunny Sunday afternoon in Prague, where the ladies weren't supposed to cross their legs above the knee.

The first half of the soccer game was almost over by the time we entered the gray, peeling, run-down stadium with rusty railings. I'd assumed the place was sold out, and was startled to see free seats everywhere, hundreds and thousands of them: the stadium was half empty — I'd been spat on and wrung through the rib-mauling mob solely because the Sparta management was grossly inept.

We sat down on the hard, wooden bench and I tried to watch the twenty-two men boot the tiny, checkered ball about the grass below. Soccer seemed such a kid's game, though, and then, very oddly, everywhere I looked, I started glimpsing familiar faces — it slowly dawned on me that the ticket seller's gray booklet covered the same rows in the same section of the main tier and that the frantic fans who, only a few minutes ago, had been madly elbowing and pushing each other, were now calmly reassembling around us to swear at the referee in two- and three-part harmony.

This Perfect Ironic Denouement to the Sparta Book of Sunday Manners made me wonder if the crazed guy wasn't sitting here somewhere too. I scanned the rows of fans, but didn't find him: he'd gone through some real panic down there and was probably still pretty shaken up.

A pretty beer vendor sauntered by and gave me something else to think about. I watched her amble down the isle with her wire holder full of white paper cups when, suddenly, a few rows below me, a guy jumped up and waved for a brew — I recognized him immediately: only some ten minutes ago, he had been hollering and spitting and clawing his way out of a tight suitcase right through me, yet now he just blindly fished some banknote out of his pocket and handed it to the vendor, not caring if it was ten crowns or a thousand crowns, for he couldn't bear to glance away from the field at all — the tiny soccer ball was the whole planet to him.

SPIRIT OF SPARTA

My Dad was a *Sparta Praha* die-hard — I grew up watching the team and hating their biggest rival, the *Slavia Praha*. In Chicago terms, Slavia was the Cubs and Sparta was the White Sox of Prague:

you couldn't root for both and you didn't switch childhood loyalties, yet when I came to Prague in 1992, Mirek Ondříček, a fervent Slavia fan, began taking me to his team's games — Slavia had a young, skilled team and they were a lot of fun to watch. I learned to know the players and began following them in the papers. And then, in the fall, Adam started playing hockey for Slavia too, and, one weekend morning, his fourth-grade team suited up against the Sparta boys.

Hockey was a game of emotion anyway and this match had the makings of a Subway World Series — the tempo was up and down and furious, kids dove into shots and checked each other viciously, but there was also biased officiating: somehow, the match was refereed by the Dad of one of the Sparta players and the guy was shameless. By the end of the first period, the parents were physically fighting in the stands. By the end of the game (which Adam's team won convincingly, and Sparta wouldn't give them a rematch all year), I'd lost my voice, my heart turned, and I was a Slavia fan.

But the arteries of my new Slavia heart were clogged with old Sparta memories. I was a renegade and it made me wonder — could that apparently senseless ticket stampede at the *Letná* stadium have carried some scrambled meaning? Was that madman in my face the Spirit of Sparta, mocking and punishing my conversion? Or was he an incarnation of some feeling of filial guilt? Wasn't the Spirit of Sparta just another haunting image of my Dad, who'd himself had his lapses of sanity? Had the stampede merely stirred up some old Oedipal emotion? Didn't they kill children in the ancient Sparta?

BOOK
OF
MEMORIES

SWEETNESS OF LIFE

For the whole year I lived there, Prague kept yanking me back to the places that no longer were — a voice frayed off the blanketing din of a crowd and brought back a long-forgotten neighbor from the Provincial Town; a girl glimpsed off a speeding train became another young woman, leaning not against a Metro wall but on a huge walnut tree, which had been cut down years ago; and the stampeding fans of Sparta at the *Letná* stadium took me back to an evening in my boyhood when I nearly got trampled for a Kilo of the Sweetness of Life.

When I was a boy, I always wanted to gorge myself on oranges, but in the Communist Czechoslovakia of the late fifties and early sixties you couldn't get tropical fruit for the life of you. The wooden crates of the "Fruits and Vegetables" shops offered pockmarked apples and pears, thick-peeled potatoes, tired carrots, garlic, and onions. An overripe fig was a thing of glamour and the oranges we got once or twice a year were greenish of color, thin of peel and big of seeds, yet eating them was always a family event: my two younger sisters and I would collect around Mom and watch her peel the orange, then carefully unglue its half-moon pieces — finally, you got to sink your teeth into a pocket of tart juice and slosh it around your mouth slowly, oohing with pleasure and smiling and sharing the moment with the beaming Mom and Dad, because Oranges Were the Sweetness of Life in the Provincial Town of Thirty Thousand Souls — when word came that a shipment of oranges had arrived in one of the fruit stores, you grabbed your shoes and you ran there pulling your coat on and you didn't tie your shoelaces till you nailed your spot in the line.

Back then, there were lines for everything: fruit, meat, books, radios, even toilet paper. And ever since I was six or seven years old, I was the designated line-stander in our family — I put a lot of thought into how you went about cutting in front of people. This was an Art for the Lion-Hearted Grounded in Practical Psychology: I'd usually amble to the head of the line as if I were looking for someone and slowly scan all the faces, reading the people as I loitered beside them, moving against the grain of the shoppers and then back again, so that everyone got used to seeing me there. Finally, I'd choose the person to merge into the line in front of: I'd look for a heavy-set older lady, dreamy with thoughts of dinner, or a shy young man with acne — you did not want to cut in front of heavily perfumed ladies or women in hats who wanted to be loud anyway or self-confident young jocks or teenage girls who had no patience or workingmen who had no time or men with fancy beards who worried about looking stupid or another kid who saw through you right away. In life, nothing was a sure thing — I got busted for crashing lines not a few times, but I also pulled off one Big Shopping Coup.

This happened at Christmas one winter while my youngest sister still believed in *Ježíšek* — there was no Santa Claus in Czechoslovakia, the Christmas Mystery operating on a higher level of abstraction there: somehow it was the *Ježíšek*, the Infant Jesus, the Naked Baby from a Stable in Jerusalem, who brought you the gifts, so you didn't get the messy contradictions about fitting tricycles through narrow chimneys and so forth. On the Eve of Christmas Day, Czech families stayed home and ate a fancy dinner of breaded carp and potato salad while *Ježíšek* fluttered about in the form of a golden pig, emitting the flickering yellow sheen that was the only physical manifestation of his presence. When the dinner was over, *Ježíšek* swooped down into the one room in the house which had been locked all day for him, for he could pass through the walls, and he dropped off the gifts and the fully decorated Christmas tree, rang a jingle bell, and was off to the neighbors.

I vividly remembered peering out the window into the cold night and smelling the factories and seeing herds of golden swine in the

sky when "GEEEEeeeenk" went the jingle bell and I raced into the
Ježíšek-baited room and there loomed a spruce, so tall it was poking
the ceiling and blazing with sparklers and candles and shining with
tinsel and ornaments — this was pure magic, because how else could
the tree and the toys, the books, the winter clothes have got there?
The door had been locked and this huge spruce wouldn't even fit
through it anyway and the candles would have been blown out by
the winter wind . . .

When my little sister was the last one of us still to believe in
Ježíšek, the whole family worked hard on protecting her Christmas
illusion. She was a clever little kid, though. "So *Ježíšek* flies right
through walls, or what?" she asked at the dinner table once.

"Oh, yes, sure! Concrete's no problem!" answered everyone.

"So can he light up candles when a hard wind is blowing too?"

"You better believe it! He can do anything at all!"

"Okay, then I want oranges for Christmas . . ."

There was a booming silence — she had reasoned us all to the
wall. Finally, Mom recovered and attempted to prepare some fall-
back options: "Oh, but what if *Ježíšek* just can't get any oranges?
What if they're out of them in the store?"

"Then he can fly to Africa and get some there."

"Well . . . Ah . . ."

"*Ježíšek can* fly to Africa, can't he?"

That year, my parents made an extra shopping expedition to
Prague, because you stood a better chance of getting lucky in a fruit
store there, but they came back empty-handed. They had started
composing their explanations when, suddenly one evening, word
came that the fruit store down the street had just gotten a shipment
of oranges — I dashed there as if I were sprinting for my life, but
found no line, only a Mob in a Christmas Shopping Frenzy pressing
toward the store door which was locked. After a while the shop manager unlocked the door and cracked it open. I couldn't see him, but I
recognized his voice: "Folks! Only the next ten customers, please!
Everyone else can go home! We're cleaned out! Ten more and that's
it, folks!"

A surge of bodies swelled toward the door. I didn't know about the
suitcase or the elephants and dove right into the free-for-all. Crouching

down, I made myself small enough to slip all the way to the door. I got kneed in the head and stepped on, but somehow became the last person to weasel my way into the closing door, past the manager who was now screaming at the top of his lungs.

The angry crowd outside wasn't dispersing; the happy crowd inside was wondering if there would be another thirty or forty kilos of oranges left to cover all the folks sardined in the shop — there was, and everyone stepped up and got his six or seven small oranges.

When the store girl let me out the back door into the cold night, I was all sweaty, the hair was freezing to my forehead, but I was flying over the sidewalk, barely touching it with my feet, soaring on the wings of adrenaline, the same wings that you sometimes grew in the movies, and then I hung the shopping bag on the outside door handle of our door and walked in and faked being disappointed for my sister's benefit. I told her I'd been late and all the oranges were gone and what a bummer it was, so that Mom could go and sneak in the shopping bag and hide the oranges on top of the wardrobe in the living room, and when we finally pulled the whole caper off, Mom secretly thanked me with her eyes and she just wouldn't quit smiling.

That was our family's last magical Christmas in the Provincial Town of Thirty Thousand Souls — the year after that even my baby sister was too old to believe in the golden pig flying to Africa to make her wishes come true, and Christmas lost all its mystery, and all the excitement of the maintenance of that mystery, and it was never the same till I had kids of my own.

CONSCIENCE CREEPING

When we arrived in Prague, everyone was still looking for spooks and their informers — the plainclothes agents of the *STB*, the ruthless State Security, had kept the Communist party in power only to melt away and seep into Czech society after the revolution. Now some ran the thugs of private security firms, called "the black sheriffs." Some drove cabs. Some used their knowledge of the old socialist economy to get filthy rich. And some leaked lists of the *STB* informers, the

Roll Call of Spooks' Little Spooks, which sold a lot of newspapers —
there were times on the Metro, when I'd lift my eyes from the page I
was reading and wonder how many of the haggard folks around me
had once been Sadistic Stalinist Spooks, how many were their Poor
Misguided Willing Pawns, how many had been strong-armed into
signing some spook pledge, and how many hadn't signed anything at
all but wound up on some list anyway, simply because a lazy spook
needed to come up with more names to earn a bonus.

It was impossible to say, because I only had a couple of encounters
with the *STB* to go on.

The first time I brushed up against the *STB* was in the winter
of 1969. A few months earlier, the Red Army had invaded Czechoslovakia to put an end to the Prague Spring and to save the country for Communism, and now a student had set himself on fire in
Wenceslas Square, prodding Prague into a spasm of political turmoil
and launching a strike by the university students.

At my *gymnasium* in the Provincial Town of Thirty Thousand
Souls, we wanted to do something too, but didn't really know what,
so we joined the university strike and groped for ideas. Finally, the
only student who could grow a beard in our school — a friend of
mine who would go on to become a writer too — declared a hunger
strike in support of the university revolt. His gesture seized everyone's imagination, but the Provincial Town's only newspaper, *Onward*,
refused to print anything about his protest, so we drafted a Fiery
Strike Proclamation, bought a bottle of kerosene, and made copies of
the statement on the school mimeograph. Several of us then divided
the town into distribution zones: the local Stalinist State Security had
been showing renewed vigor, so the proclamations had to be put up
at night, on the sly. I took the main square.

The Provincial Town started turning out its lights at about ten
o'clock every evening — I left the house at eleven: the glistening
streets were deserted and foggy. I taped the fliers mostly on the windows of the shops in the old square. I worked quickly and saw hardly
anyone. The few people that caught a glimpse of me walked faster
when they did. When I got done with the main square, I had a brilliant idea: what about the police station? Why not stick the fliers
right under the *STB* mugs?!

In the Provincial Town of Thirty Thousand Souls, the police and the *STB* shared an imposing building which overlooked a dusty, one-bench park. I headed there, excited by the idea, but kept taping up the mimeographed sheets on the shop windows in the side streets. I was getting ahead of myself though and overlooked a deep-set doorway — I had both my hands up and was fumbling with the tape when I heard two lunging steps and someone gripped me from behind.

"You son of a bitch! You're coming with me!" he barked and started dragging me toward the police station which lay only a short stretch up the street now. He had my arms pinned to my sides, so I tried twisting and kicking, but he was a bear of a man and in those days, with my winter gear on, I weighed some hundred and thirty pounds: the guy probably had a good sixty or seventy pounds on me and a lot of it was muscle — he literally lifted me up and carried me toward the police building, in a peculiar silence: I kept quiet because I didn't want the cops to hear us and I suppose that he kept quiet because he was short of breath. He didn't even holler at me when I managed to kick him in the shin with the heel of my shoe — I'd got him good though and he slammed me down and punched the back of my head with his right hand a few times, which gave me a chance nearly to twist free of his hold, so he quickly grabbed me in the bear hug again and resumed hauling me to the door of the station.

The heavy door was closed — I kicked up my feet and pushed off it with all my strength, which sent the guy staggering back, so he threw me down and pummeled the back of my head again — suddenly I realized that I was bleeding — blood was gushing down my face and burning in my eyes and there were streaks of it dripping off my chin. The guy dragged me back to the door and I lifted my legs and shoved him back once more and he slammed me down on the sidewalk and kicked me in the back. I scrambled to get away before he booted me again, but then I sensed him backing off. When I wiped the blood off my face, I saw that he was hurrying away, a big, beefy, balding man of about forty in a beige overcoat, scared off by my bleeding.

I didn't see the guy again for another three or four months. Meanwhile the cut on my head wound up being just a long scratch; all the proclamations I'd taped up got ripped down by the next morning; the student strikes petered out — it was becoming pretty clear that the Prague Spring was over, though I still didn't believe that all that energy and emotion of millions of people could simply short out, but I was a naive sixteen-year-old, thinking less with my brain than with my glands.

Life in the Provincial Town of Thirty Thousand Souls went on and soon the chestnut trees were in bloom and then, finally, the movie *A Man and a Woman* reached our cinema — the Claude Lelouch film made an extraordinary impression on my fellow citizens: single women wept quietly while the married ladies sobbed loudly, clutching their husbands — everywhere in the theater, in all its packed rows, you could feel the future generations pressing into being. No one heard the sound of one teenage mind vomiting — I saw myself as a Budding Cursed Poet back then, yet I didn't dare to let anyone sense how revolted I was by this French commercial garbage: they would have lynched me. But then on the way out, in the lobby of the theater, I collected my reward for sitting through the Lelouch drecks: a familiar face jumped out of the crowd at me — the hulking son of a bitch who had dragged me across the one-bench park was leaving the theater with a big woman in an evening gown. Her arm was coiled around his forearm and her eyes were glistening and she was in the mood in a big way.

I tailed the couple as they strolled across the bridge and into the Gothic heart of town, quite openly, twenty paces back. I fancied that my steps had the Booming Echo of a Conscience Creeping up on a Spook Thug, though I couldn't bet on it, because even after the big man noticed me, he only glanced back once or twice — I think he'd recognized me and he clearly didn't care.

He and his woman lived in an ugly shoe box of a building in the *sídliště* of the Provincial Town — I followed them right into the vestibule of it, I wanted the spook to know that I knew who he was and where he lived. As I stepped into the small lobby with mailboxes, the big man and his wife were standing on a landing, only five or six steps above me, opening the door to their first floor apartment: the wife shot me a long, probing look, but he never even glanced down — it turned out that the guy was a captain of the *STB*, which explained everything: the son of a bitch was sure I couldn't touch him and probably wanted me to know who I was dealing with.

GANJA

In 1993, Prague was full of drugs. In nightclubs, the smell of mari-huana wafted through the sweaty air. In the *Smíchov* and *Žižkov* neighborhoods, it was easy to buy hashish, LSD, opium, or cocaine. And the city was seeing its first generation of hard-core addicts — the Prague junkies shot up Pervitin, a kind of a poor man's heroin, which they called *perník,* or "ginger."

Only a dozen years earlier in Czechoslovakia, marihuana was something you only read about in the books of the Beat Poets or heard about in rock songs, and the curiosity about drugs ran high — in 1979, after I'd spent ten years abroad and become an American cit-izen, I was allowed to come back to the old country for a three-week visit, and a few days before I was to fly there, I drove to Chicago's Hyde Park and dropped in on my Jamaican Ganja Dealer.

"I need an ounce of the best shit you got," I told him.

"Cool, maaaan," the dealer flopped his dreadlocks.

"But I mean the kinda shit *you* smoke."

"Cool still."

"You're gonna open new markets in the East with it."

"Blood clot!"

My Jamaican pusher smelled a rat, but he viewed himself as a Businessman in the Global Dimension of the Word, and he came through in a spectacular fashion: a single hit off a fat spliff of his export-grade ganja had me driving the fifteen miles back home all night long, sending wonderful waves of heat down my back, my mind drifting and skipping — "You're driving!" — Since when do I talk to myself out loud? — "Concentrate!"

Every vowel packing a monstrous echo, I'd put my mind to driv-ing and realized I was flying down Lake Shore Drive at eighty miles an hour, and then, staring down the asphalted lanes, the whizzing street lamps, the park, the huge lake, the projects, I'd suddenly real-ized, "Oh, Wow! I've been here already . . . I just passed by this exit a minute ago! That's why it feels like I've been driving for hours!" But how the hell did I do that? Did I get off the Drive by mistake some-where and double back? Did I get lost in the side streets? How come I didn't remember any of this? Just because I was high? Shouldn't I recall some damn thing from such a long detour? Could this reefer be that good?

All I could be sure of though was that I'd just driven down this stretch of Lake Shore Drive, and when I tried to reconstruct my thoughts by tracking back the pinball of associations, they were like quick-moving clouds in my wind-swept mind — "Eighty miles an hour again, damn it!" — and then I'd come to again and take another close look at the road streaming by me and I'd realize: "Fuck, I've been *here* too!"

By the time I made it home, I was worn out: the clock showed I'd only been in the car for twenty minutes, but the clock lied, for every muscle in my body knew that, in one stretch, I'd just driven from sea to shining sea. The phone rang.

"So, white man?" It was the Jamaican dealer, shopping for compliments.

"Yeah, blood clot!"

"You got on that pussy yet?"

"Hey, blood clot! We're gonna open some markets with this shit! You hear me! You got my home town, man! You got everything south of the Elbe River and you got everything north of the Elbe!"

"We gotta put it in ink, white man. Wanna cruise back here, Rasta?"

I thought of the Rubber Expressway Stretching On and On between him and me: "I'm bushed, Rasta."

But his ganja was Truly Celestial: I rolled up twenty fat joints, bought a carton of Lucky Strikes, carefully undid all the cellophane wrappers, stuffed the reefers into one pack, and glued everything back together with clear glue. I bought another carton of Lucky Strikes as a decoy and told myself that you practically couldn't tell the difference between the two cartons — this was in fact One Quarter Wishful Thinking, but I was all right till I changed planes in Frankfurt: suddenly, thirty thousand feet in the air, with the Celestial To-Die-For Ganja in my suitcase, with my name on the suitcase, with the suitcase in the belly of the *Ilyushin* plane, with no more landings scheduled, I couldn't keep my mind off Murphy's First Law ("anything that can go wrong, will") or his Second Law ("I was an optimist"), or all the championship drug-sniffing canines of Czechoslovakia, or the throw-away-the-key drug sentences they passed out there, but now the die was cast.

By the time the plane landed in heavy fog in Ruzyně, I was drunk. The alcohol helped me get my nerves under control. I lifted my Ticking-Bomb Fatal Five-To-Ten-Years Suitcase off the luggage carousel and lugged it to the customs booth — the young lady officer barely gave me a second glance, so I threw the damn thing into a taxi and climbed in and just sat there and didn't even want to look at it. It was a long time before I noticed that the zipper on the suitcase had been partly undone: you could put your whole arm through the gap. I did and I felt around — both cartons of Lucky Strikes were gone.

"You ain't had no lock on that zipper?!" the cabby smirked, "Well, then the baggage handlers at Ruzyně got your cigarettes! Them goddamn rip-off artists over there will pinch your glass eye, if you're not careful!"

VAPOR AND DREAM
OF THE COLD CITY OF HARD EDGES

My three weeks in the old country in 1979 were a kind of Relentless Mild Sober Hallucination anyway. I was still writing in Czech back then, and had come to immerse myself in the healing springs of the language, to repair some of the damage it had sustained over the last decade from the Pounding Punishing Probing Priceless English. I thought I was returning to my old self, but I wound up dealing with a lot of peculiar feelings in Prague — it was beginning to dawn on me that I'd acquired another self in Chicago: I had no desire to stay anymore in the underlit, drab, dour Czechoslovakia where you constantly lowered your voice and glanced around, where everything was a problem, and where I kept tapping the back pocket of my jeans, making sure my American passport was still there and could get me back to the Cold Sky-Scraping City of Hard Edges.

And yet, I also kept suffering scary lapses of memory, as if I'd been hit on the head with a blunt instrument: there were moments when I couldn't recall my phone number or my address in Chicago, or when I'd become tongue-tied in English, or when I'd suddenly hear a horrendous accent in my voice — at times, I had the sensation of losing my Superficial Shallow False American Self as if my life in Chicago had simply dropped away from me: I couldn't imagine I had a wife and a bed and another language seven thousand miles west of Prague — the Cold Tough Chicago of Hard Edges seemed a veil of mist, an illusion, a thing of vapor and dream.

NEVER EVER? NEVER

It was during my unsettling visit to the old country that I had my second encounter with the *STB* spooks — late one morning, I was sleeping off a hangover in my aunt's apartment in Prague when a guy showed up at the door. He was about fifty years old, short, in a gray ski jacket and a brown hunting hat.

"Some American live here?" he wanted to know.

"That's me, I guess . . ." I said in Czech.

"There's something wrong with your papers, so you'll have to come with me. State Security."

It was a hollow feeling coming down the stairs of my aunt's house with the *STB* escort. I kept thinking about all the people in Kolín with whom I'd cursed the sticky-fingered baggage handler of the Ruzyně airport, wondering if the Commie Spooks had got wind of the Celestial Ganja, or what. A black Tatra 613 stood in front of the house, and I marched right to its back door, because these black limousines had figured in every *STB* story I'd ever read. I tried the handle, but the door was locked.

"What're you doin'?! That ain't mine! I didn't bring a car!" the shorty panicked.

I stepped back from the car: "Oh . . . So, what're we doing?"

"We're going to Bartolomějská Street."

Now it was my turn to be shocked: this small street with its huge *STB* building lay on the far bank of the Vltava River: "You mean you wanna walk there? On foot!?"

"Well," the shorty considered it, "we could take a streetcar too, I suppose. You got a tram ticket on you?"

Say what?! This was the *STB*? The Murderous State Security? The Vigilant Eye and the Strong Arm of the Proletariat? The Virtual Branch of the KGB? The Brain Child of Lenin and Dzerzhinsky?

"No, I sure don't," I said.

We hoofed it all the way.

The shorty seemed flattered by my mistake with the black limousine: "So you thought that was my car, huh?" he cackled, "but I told you it's just your papers, didn't I? Now if we woulda had some intentions with you, then I woulda brung a car!" — I didn't know if I should laugh or be grateful that they hadn't found out about the Celestial Ganja after all.

In Bartolomějská Street, the shorty marched me into a huge office in the gloomy building, where a man in a military shirt sat on a massive writing desk and talked on the phone. His neck was like a stove pipe, his dome was bald and tanned, he looked like a wrestler gone to seed, but he seemed quick-witted and had a big, raking laugh. A secretary entered, thumbing a file in a green folder. "We've got six pages on him," she said and handed the papers to the wrestler — this had to be my file. I was sixteen when I'd left the country, had been gone for ten years, and they still had six pages on me: now this was more like it, this was more like the Virtual KGB . . .

"Here's the American," the shorty passed me on when the wrestler finally hung up.

The wrestler studied the file for a beat: "Okay, so we're going to shorten your stay to twenty-four hours . . ."

"But why?" I said, feigning shock at being expelled from the country, though in fact I'd already figured out this was probably coming: back in the late fifties and sixties, my Dad had embezzled a million crowns from his factory's bank branch in the Provincial Town of Thirty Thousand Souls, gambled it all away, then spirited the whole family out of the country a day before his scheme busted wide open. The government had sentenced the old man to fourteen and a half years at hard labor *in absentia* — in 1979, my father was still supposed to be rotting in Czech jails and here comes Sonny Boy Strutting his Fine Leather Boots through the bars of the Provincial Town and serenading Chicago.

"We just are, that's all," the wrestler dropped down on his chair and proceeded to rummage through a drawer. He was taking out various rubber stamps, squinting at their legends, and putting them back down.

"Excuse me, but this is bullshit," I let myself get a little angry. "I am entitled to a reason. At least that."

He liked my language and gave me a friendly grin: "Okay, I'll give you a reason: it came down from the third floor." And he slapped some red stamp over my Czech visa.

"Wait a second now, please . . ." I quickly shifted gears. "You know, my time here is up anyway, I'm supposed to leave the day after tomorrow . . . Couldn't you just give me forty-eight hours?"

The wrestler flipped the page on his calendar. He was thinking about it, so I kept talking: "You know, there's a party for me tomorrow night in Kolín, so it even makes political sense. Nobody will be pissed. And I'm locked into my flight on Sunday. It'll cost me a lot of money to change it to Vienna. And . . ."

"What am I gonna do with you?" he sighed and scribbled 48 on one of the lines on his stamp.

On the way out of the office, I halted to check on one last thing with the wrestler: "So I guess I shouldn't bother applying for another Czech visa for a while, huh?"

"No," said the big guy, "You're never coming back here again."

"Never ever?"

"Never."

"But I'm not *that* old," I said. "Never is a pretty long time."

"That's a young-man kind of a thing to say," said the wrestler and we parted with smiles, because we had both liked each other's repartee — when I moved back to Prague, the city preoccupied with spooks and their informers, I often thought back on my little experiences with the *STB*. And I figured that, in these post-Communist times, the *STB* captain from Kolín was probably an embittered old pensioner, meeting with his buddies in cheap beer halls to badmouth Gorbachev, and the shorty was a night watchman in some huge bus depot of the wrestler's classy tour operation.

POETRY OF RETURNS

On that same visit but a few days before I was expelled from the country, I'd taken a walk around my old grammar school in the Provincial Town for the first time in ten years. It led to a strange encounter with a familiar face, an encounter as brief as the glimpse of a joker in a stream of shuffled cards, an encounter I wound up thinking about with some regularity for years afterwards — everything I saw during that walk seemed odd, starting with the peculiar spherical bubble looming on the dirt yard behind the school where we used to play soccer. Stuffed between the school buildings and towering over the low houses of the street, it seemed a Sight Straight Out of René Magritte.

The old dirt street in front of the school was asphalted, but the church on the far side of it, the abandoned graveyard around the church, and the stone wall around the graveyard hadn't changed at all. It looked exactly the way it had looked when, on our lunch breaks, we used to climb over it — we would steal through the high banks of dry leaves among the limestone mausoleums, pick up sticks, and dig in the dirt, the muck, and the rotten planks of old coffins inside the ancient graves: we were searching for human skulls to scare the girls with. The graves smelled richly of humus, most of them had been picked clean and we were happy to settle for a thigh bone or a rib or a clavicle. The risk you were taking on these bone-hunting expeditions was that the priest might hear you wading through the crackling drifts of leaves — this priest was still a vigorous man and he slapped you around if he ever got his hands on you.

In 1979, the graveyard wall was still covered by the old light gray mortar, speckled with mica and topped by the creepers of ivy that had always grown on it, but it seemed much smaller than it had been in my memory, where it loomed high over me: I realized I remembered it through the eyes of a seven- or eight-year-old, even though I'd climbed over it a number of times later too, when I was older and bigger — oddly, my more recent memories of the church wall had faded, while the earlier ones remained.

The wall made me think about Plankton, a schoolmate who had lived in an old stone house across the street from the graveyard. Plankton was a repeater, but he could hear you whispering a test answer to him clear across the room when you weren't even sure if you had whispered it or if you had merely thought it. The depths of his ignorance were truly unfathomable and he would grow up to be a marginal house painter, but he stuck with my class and never again repeated a grade, solely because of his bat-grade ears.

By the time we reached the seventh grade, the church too had been closed and abandoned like the graveyard, and Plankton had taken over a large mausoleum there. He made a bench from some boards and furnished it with a couple of fancy ashtrays of cut crystal. He went there to smoke and was happy just sitting there and watching squirrels, birds, a creeping cat, or a high-flying plane cutting a straight white exhaust line into the blue sky.

I didn't hang out with Plankton, but I must have gone to his smoking room a few times, because I retained an image from the mausoleum where Plankton, myself, and three or four other boys stood in a line and masturbated furiously: Plankton the year-older repeater had been boasting that he could come already, which was something everyone else in the class barely knew anything about. That lunch hour in the mausoleum, Plankton beat off for a while, then started twisting his body, his eyes were bulging as if he were about to have an epileptic seizure, and then he yelled: "Watch this!" And he came in three or four spurts right on the bench and he was so proud of himself and the stuff that had squirted out of him was gray-white and totally disgusting, but Plankton just beamed at the world, because this was the only time he got to be the first in something. The rest of us went on beating off for a while longer — without confidence that there'd be anything to show for it — and it was nothing doing yet, so we pulled our pants back up and we climbed the graveyard wall and went back to class and told the girls about the disgusting white stuff they had to look forward to in life and the girls got flushed and they giggled whenever they looked at Plankton and each time they started giggling, they couldn't stop themselves.

In 1979, as I was lollygagging past the old wall and thinking about him, Plankton suddenly appeared in the distance — as if he had been summoned by my memories. I recognized his funny, slightly spasmodic gait right away. He was ambling down the street with a couple of his work buddies in paint-splattered overalls. He hadn't changed much, still had the same sallow skin, the same huge ears on a head that was a little too large in relation to his body. He looked shocked to see me on that asphalted street: he had no doubt heard that I was in America — my father's embezzlement and our narrow escape had been big news in the Provincial Town. He gave me his old nervous grin as he strode toward me. Our meeting was the sort of encounter where you slowed down because you weren't sure if you'd stop and talk, and then it turned out that you wouldn't stop, so you speeded up again. Plankton was dragging his feet too for a few steps, clearly stricken by the same uncertainty as I was, but then we passed each other and just kept on walking — a few steps later I turned my head and there was Plankton staring back at me while continuing to saunter away.

"Hi," he said.

"Hi," I answered, but neither of us broke our stride. I looked back one more time and saw the three guys go down into Plankton's house, whose front door lay below the level of the street: Plankton was the only schoolmate I'd seen in twenty years and I saw him on a late weekend morning when time was no object, in a place as rich in memories as any spot on the planet — how strange that we hesitated briefly and walked on.

THREE LAWS OF NARRATION

There are two kinds of writing. One is drawn from experience by imagination and it's called fiction — the other comes from experience through memory and it's called nonfiction.

I began as a writer of fiction. When I turned to nonfiction I constantly had to fight the strong pull of imagination — at first glance, what I remembered always seemed too thin or drab or pointless. I wanted to fix up the recollections, to flesh them out, to make them clearer than truth, but then the peculiar distortion caused in my memories by the old graveyard wall helped me to discover the Three Laws of Narration.

The First Law was that narration always reached for meaning, whereupon the imagination supplied it — there was a relentless power that drew all narration to the fabulous. The pull of fiction, of inventing stories, of improving on real incidents, of tying them up neatly, of giving them wry endings, of making them funnier than they had been, of endowing them with the meaning they had lacked — this temptation was strong, but it had to be resisted because to give in to it was to violate the Second Law of Narration.

The Second Law of Narration was that the prosaic truth of a situation or a memory almost always contained a bigger charge of feeling than any improvements that the imagination could give it: it carried the recognition that, yes, this was how it went, this was how messy and random life got; yes, time passed; yes, feelings waned; yes, encounters happened; yes, drab and ordinary situations dragged on endlessly — but to conform to the Second Law of Narration was to break the Third Law of Narration.

The Third Law of Narration was that narration was always based on memory, and memory always reached for meaning — when I remembered the graveyard wall across the street from my school as tall and looming over me, I remembered it through the eyes of a seven-year-old, for whom scaling it was a challenge and for whom the priest lurked in the graveyard, protecting the bones of his dead. I didn't remember it the way it was when I was thirteen, after it had shrunk in relation to me, after I'd easily swing over it to masturbate in the mausoleum that Plankton had furnished with ashtrays.

So memories always lied, but they lied the truth. They were chronological fictions, but they contained deeper emotional verities: graveyard walls blew back up in size; the dead got younger and they lingered looking the way they had been when you had loved them or hated them or feared them the most — memories were the true fictions, and great books had to be like memories, where every character found his or her right age, where all things were loaded with their greatest emotional charge, and where all encounters just happened.

ACTIVE INGREDIENTS

In writing this book, I took heart from the fact that memory is itself a kind of an imagination.

BOOK
OF
WRITERS

FAT ENVELOPE

I intended to support the family with my writing in Prague, and I finally did, by shopping the Forman autobiography around and selling it to the highest bidder. The book became a best-seller and paid most of our bills.

There was also a considerable interest in my first American novel, *The Willys Dream Kit*, which had already been beautifully translated into Czech by Jaroslav Kořán. (Kořán too had taken a memorable ride on the Roller Coaster of Revolutionary Fortunes: back in the Long Hours of the Short Velvet Revolution when people were buttonholed in hallways and given big jobs, Kořán got appointed the mayor of Prague. He was fired from the job less than two years later and happily became the editor of the Czech edition of *Playboy*.) Eager Czech publishers had been writing and courting me across the Atlantic Ocean — my only problem was I had an agent in Prague.

Right after the revolution, I'd signed on with the first literary agency in the country, which was a brain child of Václav Havel. The president's outfit immediately collected a Gang of Czech Literary Heavy-Hitters, and I was glad that I could join this Talent-and-Lit-Fame Cartel. But then the agency had my books and months started turning into years and nothing was happening — and even after we moved to Prague, after I chose a publisher for *The Willys Dream Kit* myself and told the agent merely to wrap up the contract, the agency still couldn't clinch the deal — they immediately got into a tiff with the publishing house, a snide affair having to do with obscure punctuation lapses in each other's contracts and letters.

An agent in the West couldn't afford such pettiness: you had to cultivate publishers and editors; you had to know the market; you had to keep a strong author list; and you had to be in the office. My Czech agents had no idea how much novels were bringing in the chaotic book market; they corrected the editors' grammar instead of wining and dining them; they threw parties for their own authors, rather than new talents; and when I stopped by their office during the week, the person I needed to see usually wasn't there.

Once I dropped the agency, it took only a week to close the *The Willys Dream Kit* deal with Atlantis, a publishing house based in the city of Brno and run by one Mrs. Uhde, who offered to wire the advance to my bank account.

"No, no, no," I quickly told her, because I'd heard that Czech banks took up to two months to release the funds, "I want cash. I'll drive to Brno and get it, if I have to."

"Oh, no, that won't be necessary," Mrs. Uhde told me, "I'll take care of it."

A few days later, I found myself under the gilded ceiling of a corner office of one of the most powerful politicians in the land. There were a couple of flagship desks floating in a deep-carpet sea and several touch-tone phones singing like mermaids. The man had two efficient secretaries and an oily factotum of an aide. He had strolled up, given me a firm handshake, and taken me into his office. He had closed the door behind us. He had reached into the breast pocket of his fine suit and handed me a fat envelope.

"You'd better count it," he said.

I ripped the sealed envelope open: "This is how things get done in Chicago, too." He laughed and I counted the thick stack of well-thumbed money. "Then they find you in the lake with cement boots on," I went on entertaining him, "or somebody smells you in a trunk of a stolen car that's been standing in a parking garage for a week."

The money was all there. We did a little more small talk, and then I headed home and, one by one, slipped the banknotes between the pages of my Webster's dictionary which was my bank in Prague — I figured the Czech burglars rarely needed to look up an English word and I knew that, in the event of a fire, the Webster was one of the first things I'd grab.

SHOES TO COMMUNISM

The powerful politician was the Chairman of the Czech Parliament and a writer in his own right. His name was Milan Uhde and he was the husband of my publisher — the envelope contained my Atlantis advance in cash.

After the Velvet Revolution, under the Dissident Jailbird Playwright President Václav Havel, the Czech government had a number of artists in it, but most of them soon got out of politics again — they had found the enterprise too tedious, hypocritical, and too much work. Milan Uhde stayed in. He joined the winning political party of Václav Klaus right when it was forming and, as a former playwright, brought his sense of the theater to bear on the pedestrian life of the Czech legislature.

Shortly after he slipped me the fat envelope in the Parliament building, I ran into Uhde again at an opening night party in the bar of the National Theater, where he was now sitting in a bubble of Us-Against-Them Cut-the-Politician Isolation — I made a point of greeting him, and he grabbed me and sat me down at his table. It wound up being a rather long night: we drank beer and Uhde talked. There was a pent-up verbal energy in the man, as if he hadn't unwound like this in a long time. He was a fine raconteur, slipping in and out of characters, accents, and dialects, which were always dead on. He told Emperor-Is-Naked Stories about the struggles with the inane Communist censors in the sixties and he rendered episodes from the lives of the famous artists of Brno. He knew Milan Kundera well (Atlantis was putting out all of Kundera's books in Czech) and had once worked at a literary magazine under the great Czech poet Jan Skácel who wrote:

> it's up in the andes or slightly under
> a white quarry a white lama
> a white piano missing keys
> with Mr. Thunder banging on the ivories

Skácel's work was hard to translate: it was musical and plainspoken at the same time, lyrical and playful and true:

knees to the old chin
as if back in Mom's belly oh
go sheep I'm counting on you go
across this night of gin

I was curious to hear any gossip about the man and it came as
a surprise when Uhde told me that, like many of his contempo-
raries, Skácel had started out as a True Blue Communist — I hadn't
known that, because Skácel's Hack Socialist-Realist poems hadn't
been included in the notorious anthology of embarrassing poetry
from the fifties I'd read a few years earlier. The book, which had
been maliciously published and gleefully read, contained a memorable ode on Stalin by youthful Milan Kundera and a load of Over-
the-Top Drop-Dead-Shameful poems of Pavel Kohout, but nothing
from Skácel's pen.

"Well, that's because the editors of the anthology loved Skácel, so
they gave him a break," explained Uhde and he recited Skácel's own
ode on Stalin. The poem was silly enough to make the book all right,
full of Georgian apples and shawls and mountain streams, but it was
also intricate and very long. Uhde recited the whole thing, strophe
after strophe, quatrain after quatrain — the chairman of the Parliament clearly had a fine memory, but he also must have been quite
taken by Skácel.

I understood why when he told me how, out of the blue one afternoon, while drinking fine Moravian wine, the great poet started
describing his Road to Communism — Skácel came from a very poor
region of Moravia, his father was a head teacher, and Skácel "was
the only kid in the village who owned a pair of shoes . . ." The boy
begged his parents to let him walk barefoot like all the other kids,
but they wouldn't hear of it: "Your lungs are weak! You're suscep-
tible to pneumonia! And you *do* have a pair of shoes! And you're
keeping them on period!"

And so Skácel's shoes became his guilt-ridden ticket to Communism, and, who knows, maybe to poetry too:

there's so much sadness you need a crane
to lift it a truck to haul it to the shore

a whale to build you a house of it
and three hundred years to open the door

WORDS AND MONEY

Before the Velvet Revolution, in the days of the Late Anemic Communism, American writers visiting Prague would regularly suffer a
pleasant embarrassment there. William Styron, John Updike, Kurt
Vonnegut, and Arthur Miller had probably sold more hard-cover
books in the tiny country of Czechoslovakia than they had in the
Sea-to-Shining-Sea Book-Club Readers-Group America.

Back then, the Czechs would read everywhere they went and they
read voraciously. Every Thursday, long lines formed in front of all
the bookstores, because that was when the new books came out. The
language had only ten million speakers, but a popular author could
count on the first edition to run in six figures. The works of a great
and beloved writer, someone like Bohumil Hrabal, sold in millions.
And all this came on top of the underground world of publishing, an
Anthill of Nocturnal Behind-Closed-Doors House-Search-Courting
Activity, where the real Czech literature was surviving.

While in the West, intriguingly, a critic calculated that the number of serious readers amounted roughly to the cube root of the
population, in the Communist Prague even blue collar people had
read books, for literature was vicariously doing the job of politics,
pornography, history, philosophy, anthropology, sociology, psychology . . .

The End of Communism put an end to this Golden Age of Letters. Book stalls sprung up in subway stations and on street corners, but instead of selling poetry or fiction, their youthful operators
hawked sensationalist bios of the stars of rock 'n roll or the vampires
of Communism, how-to books, and pornography. At the same time,
in a one-two knockout combination, tabloids arrived — the newspaper with the widest circulation in the Czech Republic was called
Blesk or "Flash." Its thick headlines tugged thin articles, its colorful
type screamed alarmist revelations, and there was a quota of air-
brushed nudes.

Under post-Communism, the sales of literary works plummeted. The prints of first editions dropped by a factor of ten. The sale of five thousand copies which had once been considered poor for a book of poetry now became the benchmark of commercial success for a novel — Czech publishing had caught up with the rest of the Western world in a hurry.

None of this had surprised me. I'd been living in a country where not even the cube root of population read, but I felt sorry for the Czech writers and, in a strange way, ashamed. It was quite dumb on my part to feel this way: didn't I know the planet was sick and literature was dying? Wasn't the value of words clearly dropping while the value of images kept climbing? Didn't I realize it all had to happen in Prague too? So why did I suddenly find it tough to go and see Bohumil Hrabal?

BOHUMIL HRABAL

Bohumil Hrabal was the most popular writer in Czechoslovakia, both with the reading public and other writers. He had a great following in France, Spain, Italy, and Germany, too, but in English he never found a congenial translator.

Some writers processed the world through the eye, some through the ear — Hrabal had both a superb ear and a superb eye. He was well versed in classical philosophy, with a doctorate in law, which he claimed he was sparing no effort to make himself forget. A master stylist who had started out as a poet, he wrote entertaining fiction, driven by manic rhythms and exploding with fireworks of brilliant metaphors. And he had the wisdom to stay close to home in his writing — both his parents, his Motor-Mouth Uncle Running-on Apple-Strudel Sentences, and his German-born wife had become famous personages in Czech letters.

"A writer should be humble, he should live roughly the way the other people live . . ." Hrabal once described his writing ethos in an interview, "If possible, he shouldn't live in luxury . . . When my Grandma and Grandpa got married, they had: Grandma — an alarm clock, so they could get up on time, and Grandpa: a half-liter beer mug. I started out the same way. And that's what it's about, it's a question of being common in a way, of suppressing yourself so that you don't wind up surrounded with certain comforts, bookcases and central heating and so on . . . You could say that I was a rich man now, but I spend most of my time in Kersko, in my cottage, where the only water I have is the water that I pump up out of the ground . . . And I lug it in buckets like all the regular folks used to do it . . . I do things the old way, I get at them through the tactile sensation and impression, everything passes through me, I see my water, I pump my water up, I lug it around in those buckets. These are all apparently little things, but I live off them . . ."

Hrabal didn't begin to live off his writing till he was well into his forties. He had worked at a provincial railroad station during the war, sweated in the foundries of Kladno after the Communist revolution of 1948, had been a stagehand for several years, had scrapped forbidden books while running a paper-recycling press. All the while, he conducted his life in bars and taverns. He took buses and went to soccer games with everyone else, and wrote about it on an old manual typewriter. And he embraced the streets, canteens, dead-end jobs, bars, hospitals, soccer stadiums, the whole of the Czech life, investing this God's plenty in all its murderous and poetic forms with a mythical monumentality — the one belief that ran through all his writing held that anything that existed was beautiful, simply because it was.

Hrabal's creative temperament had always been Dionysian. He had communed with the surrealists at different points in his life and his writing method owed something to their working style. He would look, listen, think, and patiently collect images, ideas, scraps of dialogue, feelings; he'd let them stew in his subconscious; he'd wait till he was filled to bursting with them. Then came the purging flood — his major works had been written in short bursts of Intense, Subconscious-Driven, Light-Headed, World-Falling-Away, Machine-Gun salvos, with mauled typewriter keys chopping into one another and stacking up, with sheets of paper just rolling through his machine — "at times the flow-rate of paper through my typewriter clocked eight minutes a sheet." Early in his career, he would rewrite his texts five or six times, and later he preferred to work *"alla prima"* — but the books were always stunning.

Whenever I found myself in Prague, I tried to pay Hrabal a visit. He was an old man when I first met him — he was born in 1912 — and had been living a life of habit for years, so he was always easy to find. He had buried his wife and many of his old friends and never had any children. He lived alone in a modest two-room apartment in the working neighborhood of *Vysočany*. Every morning, he bought some ground beef, got on a diesel bus, and headed to his cottage in the woods of Kersko.

The boxy two-story structure stood under tall pines, beside a well with a manual pump. Hrabal kept his cats there, sixteen of them at the last count — his beloved, silky black tom Cassius too a fixture of Czech literature. He would pet and feed the cats, then write and read for most of the day. In the afternoon, he'd get on another bus for the hour-long ride back to Prague.

On most evenings of the week, Hrabal could be found in the small back room of an Old Town pub, called "Golden Tiger," which served the golden, creamy, foamy Pilsner Urquell beer. Its guests were fiercely territorial — "That joint's like a synagogue," the young poet Jáchym Topol described it once to me, "Everybody has his own chair there . . ."

Hrabal held court at the head of a barren, pine-wood table for a dozen admirers. Some were intellectuals, some bore tattoos, some had come a long way to see him: translators, Bohemists, foreign fans, freaks — "this guy has killed a cop," Hrabal introduced a strapping Slovak to me once. For three or four hours he listened, sniffed tobacco, talked, and signed books. He sampled the home-made culinary delights that people brought him and drank beer. He sang or recited long passages from Yesenin or Apollinaire. And then, between seven and eight in the evening, the bartender called Hrabal a cab. By then the old writer had usually downed four, six, sometimes ten big steins of beer and the poor circulation in his legs made them hurt. He would collect his little University of Chicago back-pack, pay the tab — for everyone, usually — and go home to a sleepless night.

GO TO HELL

"I'm taking you guys to maybe the greatest writer you'll ever see in your lives," I told my kids one evening in the summer of 1992 and I took them to the Golden Tiger.

Adam and Sonja peered curiously at the vigorous old man, wide of chest and wider of cheekbone — "I've got Tartar blood in me, just look at the width of this mug" — with the hands but not the belly of a working man. A rim of gray hair framed his ruddy bald pate and the blue eyes took you in briefly, then looked away, then gazed at you again. Even when he fell silent, everyone in the bar deferred to him.

We'd brought Hrabal a Chicago Bulls cap — the Bulls had just won their second World Championship in basketball — and he beamed, put it on his head, ordered that room be made for us beside him at the crowded table, then bought us a dinner even though we'd just eaten at home.

"Michael Jordan!" he said. He had been watching the NBA finals which Czech television broadcasted live at the crack of dawn. "What an incredible personality!" Most of the intellectuals at the table had only a vague notion of what he was talking about, but my kids smiled and nodded happily. "'Even my mistakes are perfect!'" Hrabal quoted Jordan, "now there's a sentence . . . It would take Nietzsche a couple of days of hard work to come up with that. And me, I can't work that hard anymore myself. These little essays I'm writing nowadays, I piss 'em out in a couple of hours!"

"Bohumil, that's the last book of yours that I'll ever publish!" said a youthful man with lively eyes, an enormous beard, and a barrel-sized body. He was the owner of Pražská Imaginace which had been bringing out Hrabal's latest works — for Hrabal kept writing. A thin paperback of his ruminations, *The Aurora Aground*, had just come out.

The old man no longer rewrote anything. He was mixing philosophy with a sort of impressionistic journalism of the self — the voice remained unmistakable, but the writing no longer possessed the force of a hammer blow between the eyes: Hrabal had finally reached the stage in his career when he was beyond editorial protection from himself, but in this case, it didn't matter. He had written his great books, he had earned the right to do as he damned well pleased, and he was doing just that — lately he had been giving away shopping bags full of cash.

The second time I went to see Hrabal that year, he marched me out of the Golden Tiger and across the street into a restaurant for dinner. We sat in the depths of a noodle-shaped room by a cool wall of medieval masonry and, as if through a tunnel, watched the brilliant powder of sunlight dust the bustling street — the light was northern and slanted and the shadows of tourist carriages and horses and women in summer dresses were long and thin, almost transparent. "You're coming home with me tonight, I want to give you twenty grand for those kids of yours," Hrabal told me, "I just don't have the cash on me right now."

"No, thank you," I said, "you know I'm an American . . ."

He didn't like that. We talked about Czech writers and he didn't like most of the people I liked and, by the end of the evening, Hrabal told me to go to hell — that was another thing that Hrabal was doing a lot of in his old age, sending everyone to hell.

When I was leaving Prague, I went to say good-bye to the old master. It was an odd feeling, for you never knew if you'd ever see him again. I found him in another beer hall near the Old Town Square, surrounded by his old pals, munching on open-faced sandwiches of pumpernickel, goose lard, pickles, and paprika.

"Now you show up, after I've had six beers," Hrabal welcomed me gruffly, but he was glad to see me. A new book of his had just come out, *A Good Night Story for Cassius,* another thin paperback of insomniac ruminations, and Hrabal called the waiter over and ordered a beer and a book for me. The waiter brought the book from a tidy stack displayed in the niche by the bar. He jotted its price down on Hrabal's bill as if it were a plate of goulash. The old man wrote an affectionate dedication on the title page, then started rummaging in his backpack. He slowly fished out a pair of scissors, a tube of glue, and an envelope with a few xeroxed sheets.

"They dropped my postscriptum from the book," he said.

As usual, the publisher was sitting by his far elbow. "In this case, it was no big loss," he defended himself.

"You go to hell, sir," said Hrabal.

"That's the last book of yours I'll ever publish," said the publisher.

"Go to hell," said Hrabal.

It was all in good nature, perfectly timed, a comedy routine. The postscriptum was only a couple of paragraphs long — a single xeroxed sheet contained several of the missing addenda, so Hrabal carefully cut one out. He unscrewed the top of the tube of glue and smeared the back of the clipping with it. He pasted it on the last page of the text with precision. He shut the paperback. He lifted himself off the bench. He slipped the book under him and dropped down on it.

"A couple quick beers and it's ready," he said.

Here was the greatest writer Czech literature had sitting on his latest book — we sipped beer and waited for the cheap glue to dry. "These days, six beers and I'm through with conversation," Hrabal informed me, so we didn't talk much. The old man had pumped his own water all his life and given away shopping bags of cash and sent everyone to hell, and he glued his last words into his last book for me, and it was a fine feeling.

PLAYFUL PRESIDENT

At the time, Bohumil Hrabal was not Prague's best known writer, but the city's Most Famous Author had given up writing — Václav Havel was still the president of Czechoslovakia when we arrived in Prague, concluding his first term in office, his What-the-Hell Try-Anything-Once Playful Playwright's Presidency. He was still an artist, a writer subverting the Pompous Pretensions of Presidential Decorum, and having a ball doing it. Back then, Havel didn't intend to stay in politics and didn't bother to behave like a politician.

This playwright and essayist had come to the job completely unprepared. He had, for the previous twenty years, lived on the margins of Czech life or in prison, taking moral positions which freaked out most of his fellow citizens — not without reason, because Havel himself had nearly paid for them with his life: in the early eighties, both his lungs collapsed in a prison hospital and he nearly died there. But he had a quiet, self-effacing doggedness in him that never quit and, when Communism finally died with a whimper, he was the country's only viable candidate for the first post-Communist presidency.

During Havel's first year in office, my closest friend in the country, Joska Skalník the abstract painter, served Havel as the Presidential Advisor for Cultural Matters at Hradčany Castle, so I've heard in gripping detail what a Rock-'n-Rolling Wild-and-Crazy Whale-of-a-Time it was — Havel set the tone for his administration as soon as he was sworn in: he donned a U.S. Army jacket and made for the Old Town Square where he celebrated his election with the people, tens of thousands of them, getting his back slapped and boogying and chugging drinks straight from the bottles that were passed to him.

In those days, the long-haired Havel still wore sweaters, chain-smoked on global television, and surrounded himself with old friends from the underground: screenwriters, theater directors, rock musicians, and painters. He hung out with Frank Zappa and the Dalai Lama. He talked about "apolitical politics" and invented slogans such as "Truth and Love Shall Vanquish Lies and Hate" (a riff on the percussive "Truth Vanquishes" of the fourteenth-century Czech faith-warrior Hussites). He was awarded doctorates by famous universities and gave speeches about how he wasn't educated enough to deserve them, how guilty and inadequate they made him feel.

For the first time in twenty years, Havel's plays were produced in Prague again. He went and enjoyed himself at their openings — all the jauntiness of that time is conveyed by his quip to Jaromír Vodička, the director of the Balustrade Theater, where, back in the sixties, Havel had honed his playwrighting craft: "Mr. Vodička, I bet that thirty years ago, when you were hiring me as a stagehand here, it hadn't occurred to you that one day I'd abolish the Warsaw Pact!"

Havel refused to move to Hradčany Castle, which was the Czech White House. "The first time we went on an inspection of the grounds of the Castle," Joska told me, "we nearly pissed ourselves laughing . . . All those saunas and sofas and bars, the pool Husák had put in, all that gravy of power seemed so absurd, so unnecessary, so crazy." And so the first post-Communist president stayed across the river from the Castle, in the old, cramped apartment which he shared with his brother's family.

In the spring of 1990, several months after the Velvet Revolution had lifted Havel to the presidency, an ABC film crew gumshoed up an old tower across the street from Havel's apartment and found two gray-haired men there, with lunch boxes and surveillance gear. The men turned out to be a couple of work-a-day *STB* spooks, still reporting to their job, which had for years been to spy on Arch Dissident and Enemy of the State Havel — the man had, in the meantime, become the State, but no one had called these two spooks off their out-of-sight out-of-mind job that had paid well for years, so they went on spying on him.

When Jackie Judd, the ABC correspondent, told the president about the on-going State Security stake-out she had uncovered across the street from his house, Havel laughed and said: "Well, it certainly doesn't surprise me . . ." And he let it go at that — he didn't take names and kick ass: he was used to this and it didn't bother him.

At times, it even seemed as if the new president was having trouble distinguishing between the old *STB* and his new Secret Service — he kept toying with his security detail mercilessly. "Václav loved to stop the presidential caravan by some village pub buzzing with flies and flash that shit-kicking grin of his and say: 'Let's go get a beer'," Joska reported, "So one time we're in this village pub and Václav comes up to me and says: 'You wanna see something? Follow me!' And he leads me into the back room and climbs right out this open window . . . We were a couple of hundreds meters down the road before the dicks noticed that the president's gone — you should've seen them scramble and freak!"

Another favorite pastime of the Playful President and his Hradčany Gang were the surprise inspections of sundry state enterprises — none of them had been privatized yet, so Havel was still their Supreme Boss: "One day, we were supposed to ambush this collective farm," Joska recounted. "The place had been a Communist showcase and our trip was super secret, a soul wasn't supposed to know . . . We even gave the security detail a bogus itinerary. Then, on the way to this bogus destination, we suddenly veer off and make for that collective farm. So the presidential caravan screams into the village, the hens scatter, the dogs are barking, Václav swings the door of his BMW open and springs out and — a brass band cuts on! The chairman of the collective is standing there with a tray of slivovitz shots!" Joska knew right then "that the gig was up ..."

When the painter and Oscar-winning costume designer Dóda Pištěk designed uniforms for the Hradčany guard, Havel liked their toy-soldier look so much he promoted the reservist private to the rank of a colonel — "you shoulda seen the faces of the generals of the High Command drop! Man, they got longer than an aardvark's snout!" Joska told me.

Havel also had a great time hosting his old underground buddies in the stately presidential retreat of Lány. Pavel Landovský, the great actor, had spent a weekend with his long-time Beer-and-Room-Theater companion Havel: "So that first morning, Havel runs out, jumps into one of the brand new BMWs, and starts tooling around the estate. He roars up to me, stomps on the brakes, skids to a halt, and yells: 'Watch this!' And he floors the gas pedal and spins the wheels ... These geysers of mud are shooting through the air, the tires are screeching, and the president is grinning from ear to ear like a kid who just pinned a donkey tail on a cop."

It was around that time that Havel prepared to go to Moscow to meet with Mikhail Gorbachev, then still the Big Heat of the Big-Brother Soviet Union, which hadn't yet pulled the tens of thousands of its Red Army troops out of Czechoslovakia. The two leaders had exchanged handwritten letters and Havel was clearing his desk before the trip. He still had to take care of a slight political embarrassment — some old man had declared a hunger strike to protest the post-Communist government's "coddling" of the Germans and he was sitting right on Wenceslas Square and getting acres of print in all the papers.

"Finally Havel had to invite the old man to his office," Joska told me. "Václav sat him down right at the presidential desk and the old guy just ate up all the attention ... It took about five minutes to get him to promise that he'd start stuffing his face again ..."

The next morning, several advisors were standing around Havel's office at Hradčany Castle when security called from downstairs:

"That geezer that was on that hunger strike is back!" So Havel turned to Joska and said: "Now what does he want? Can you go down and see?"

When Joska met with the old man, "he was white as a sheet, practically shaking, mumbling incoherently: 'I'm sorry, sir, I really didn't mean to do that, I dunno how it happened, I am so sorry, sir, I apologize . . .'" And he handed Joska a sheet of paper. "So I look at it," reported Joska, "and man! — it's Gorbachev's personal, handwritten letter to Havel!"

In his salivating elation over getting off the hunger strike, the old man had somehow picked up the letter off the presidential desk and stuck it in his pocket. And now he was terrified that he had put a crimp in the Czech-Soviet relations right as the country was trying to get rid of the Red Army troops — Joska calmed him down, sent him back home, and ran upstairs to the presidential office giggling. Havel was still there, talking to a guy in a suit.

"Damn, Václav! You're not gonna believe this, but that old man lifted your personal letter from Gorbachev yesterday! Here it is," said Joska, but he saw that Havel had a very strange look in his eyes, and then he realized that the man in a suit too was staring at him "as if he were a mouse that's just been plowed up."

The suit was the Soviet ambassador.

TYPEWRITER TERROR

All good things must come to an end, even in public life. The Czech voters delighted in having a Coyote-in-the-Henhouse Playful President, but then, slowly, the perception that Havel wasn't taking care of business set in — "Yes, Havel had gone all over the world and put us on the map and all that," a radio editor told me when we arrived in Prague, "but here at home, he had left everything up to "Love and Truth" and they just didn't do the job. None of the fat Communists had been punished. In fact, they all got fatter."

In July of 1992, Slovak nationalists blocked Havel's re-election to the presidency of the Czecho-Slovak Federal Republic, and he swiftly resigned. Seven months later, after Czechoslovakia had split into the Czech and Slovak republics, Havel regained the presidential chair and moved back into Hradčany Castle, but he was a different man, in a different country, with a different conception of the job: Havel's second term was a Get-Back-to-You No-Comment The-Time-Is-Up Politician's Presidency — in Prague's history, this metamorphosis ranked right up there with that of Kafka's Georg Samsa: how did it happen? Was the playwright always really a politician? And if not, when did he realize what was happening to him? Was he, in his own mind, ever clear on what he wanted? Did he just become a politician by default?

Some of Havel's old buddies from the dissident underground felt betrayed by the metamorphosis. They delighted in documenting how Havel repeatedly said one thing and then did another — right before the revolution, dissident Havel gave an interview to an underground newspaper and said that "politics was a terrain that I shall never tread on." He even flatly declared he wouldn't take the presidency, even if he were offered the job. Later, after he first became president, he kept talking about how he longed to get back to his typewriter and how he would serve only till the next election. Still later, when he stood for preserving Czechoslovakia, he declared he wasn't interested in presiding over a truncated part of it, and so on.

With a record like his, most politicians would have been history. Havel managed to hold on to the presidency, though he did wind up being a much weaker leader of a lot smaller country — what had actually happened to Havel the writer? How could the tiny politician inside the artist swallow his host? Had all those caravans of limos, the guards, the fancy address, the summer houses, the fellow statesmen, the elbowing pack rats, the Blank Pages of History, that gleam in people's eyes, merely got the better of a fine man? Did Havel merely demonstrate that he was only human? Did he prove Lord Acton right? Did power always corrupt? And did absolute power always corrupt absolutely? Was it so hard to walk away from Being a Global Player? Or was the man just terrified of his typewriter? And if so, why was he so terrified? Was it because life was elsewhere?

LIFE IS ELSEWHERE

The only truly world-famous Czech writer was not very well known in Prague. The novelist Milan Kundera had left the country in the seventies and he was living a reclusive life in Paris, where he was experimenting with French.

In 1992, the Czech public had yet to see Kundera on television, because, publicly, he had never come back. (He had in fact slipped into Brno for a couple of brief, incognito visits.) His early books were remembered only by the older generations. And his great novels were yet to be published in the country. (Kundera was wisely releasing his old novels in an unhurried, chronological order — he had watched how, in the post-revolutionary euphoria, all the banned Czech authors had rushed all their banned books to the readers, and ended up dissolving their work of twenty years in a Sudden Flash-Flood Glut of Words . . .)

No one in Prague knew my favorite Kundera book, a novel from the early seventies, called *Life is Elsewhere*. It was a story of a lyrical poet who became a police informer and wound up turning in his lover to the State Security, whereupon Kundera dispatched the poet with a Grotesque Sissy Death, making him freeze on a balcony while wearing ridiculous boxer shorts.

The book was a *roman à thèse*, its thesis being that lyrical poets were jerks. Kundera illustrated his contention brilliantly with stories from the Lives of Great Poets. He suggested that artists were Inadequate Neurotics with Screwed-up Lives, who created Beauty as a compensation for their own lack of human grace. Life was elsewhere and they longed to join its stream, but when they got up their nerve and attempted to become players, they always wound up only falling on their faces.

Kundera usually wrote from the head, but *Life is Elsewhere* had clearly come out of his gut: I thought that he was looking back at his own Talent-Dripping Youthful Self which had been capable of writing an ode on Stalin while, in the same city, Stalin's victims were swinging off the gallows. He had always been the Powerful Poet of Shame, Disgust, and Embarrassment: people rarely ate or drank in his books; the clothes they wore mostly made them feel ridiculous;

they had a lot of sex, but the biggest erotic charge came from shame and humiliation — strangely, Kundera's closest psychological relation in the literary family seemed to be Jonathan Swift, for the psychic motor of *Life is Elsewhere* ran on self-disgust, yet there was no denying the novel's punch — *Life is Elsewhere* was that rare instance of a deeply felt cerebral book.

But if Kundera was right and if, for an artist, Life really was elsewhere, then for the men of action, Art had to be elsewhere too — and didn't Stalin and Mao fail as poets? Didn't Hitler and Churchill try to paint? Didn't Reagan try to act?

It seemed true: you were either outside of Life or you were outside of Art, and Kundera's insight went a long way to explain the predicament that Havel and the other Artist-Politicians in Prague were struggling with, for until the Velvet Revolution, Life certainly *was* elsewhere for the Dissident Room-Theater Live-In-Truth Havel. The revolution, however, thrust him into Life — he became a president, a public figure, a man of action, and gradually he departed from the elsewhere of Art.

And yet, a writer who became a public figure paid a price for his metamorphosis — there was a certain sensitivity that came with not fitting in, an awareness, a vulnerability that politicians didn't have or couldn't show, a keener sense of life that came from constantly being rubbed raw by it, the strength of always doubting yourself, the strength of a lack of satisfaction and confidence, the distorting but revealing optics of neuroses, the wisdom of a sense of inadequacy — in Kundera's view, these were the sources of great art. Clearly, a national leader, a statesman who was waited on by others, dressed by consultants, coached by image-makers, fawned over by society ladies, and flattered by toadies would quickly get over such a vulnerability — maybe Havel hadn't even noticed it at first. His first presidency was a lot of fun and he didn't behave like a politician, but as time went on and he clung to the office while still talking about getting back to Art, you began to wonder: didn't Havel realize that leaving Life was going to be harder than leaving Art had been? And that there weren't going to be any revolutions to propel him back? Didn't he know that the only way to get back to Art was to leave the presidential office in utter disgrace?

BOOK
OF
DIVORCE

LOGIC OF STATECRAFT

What does it take to make a country? A war. What does it take to break a country? A fat and a skinny politician. When does a country bust? At the stroke of midnight. And who cares?

BAG OF ONIONS

On January 1, 1993, at 0000 hours, Czechoslovakia split into the Czech and Slovak republics, an event which had been foretold to me some fifteen years earlier, though I hadn't paid attention, for the augury happened in the pet food section of a Jewel Food store in Berwyn, Illinois.

Late one evening back in the seventies, I was making a cat food run to a supermarket when a guy came around a distant corner of a deserted isle and strode toward me. He was slinging a bag of onions over his shoulder and I realized that I knew him: he was a fellow immigrant, an unemployed Slovak I'd just met a couple of months earlier at the gas station of my mechanic.

He had been sitting around the garage drinking the mechanic's beer when I dropped off my car, and later gave me a ride home in the mechanic's Mercedes. He seemed like a nice guy. We didn't have a whole lot to talk about, but we talked easily. He let me off in front of my house; I thanked him and never gave him another thought.

In the supermarket, the Slovak showed no sign of recognizing me as I halted to say hello. I never got the words out — "Czech swine!"

he growled suddenly and whacked me over the head with his bag of onions. I was so shocked I just froze and stared: didn't I have a can of cat food in my hand? Why hadn't I popped him right back? I just stood there — the guy rushed off and I never saw him again.

The mechanic was a Slovak too and he laughed so hard when I told him about his chauvinist buddy he had to lean forward to catch his breath.

SAME DIFFERENCE

As languages went, Czech was closer to Slovak than Spanish was to Portuguese, but the Czechs and the Slovaks were clearly two different peoples — back under the Habsburg monarchy, hadn't the Better Czechs spoken German even while the Better Slovaks spoke Hungarian? Didn't few of the ironic Czechs believe in God? And didn't the Slovaks have Catholicism in their blood, whether or not they went to church on Sunday? Didn't the Czechs drink beer? Didn't the Slovaks drink wine? And didn't the national temperaments reflect what went into the liver?

And yet, in 1992, the old marriage in the house of Czechoslovakia didn't seem on the rocks any more than the similar unions in Canada or Belgium: the polls in Slovakia consistently showed that less than a third of the population wanted to split Czechoslovakia — arriving in Prague in the summer of 1992, despite having been whacked over the head by a bag of onions, I still didn't fully get the bottom line of the Slovak separatism. For the past twenty-three years in Chicago, Slovaks had been fixing the brakes on my car and playing house-league hockey with me and drinking till dawn afterward with the greatest of ease — I finally asked Roman Polak to explain the rift in the country to me.

Polak was a tall, elegant Slovak with a curtain of long hair around a bald dome, who dressed in long black coats and wide-brim hats. He had once been the junior champion of Slovakia in the 400-meter hurdles — a particularly punishing race for which he had trained "the kamikaze way: I tried to knock myself out in every practice . . ."

Now he was bringing the same attitude to the theater: at the age of thirty-five and in full command of all elements of his art, he was directing plays at the National Theaters of both Prague and Bratislava.

Like most Slovak intellectuals, Polak wasn't thrilled by the prospect of the break-up of the country, yet when I asked him if he'd ever felt like a second-class citizen in Czechoslovakia, he told me: "Maybe not a second-class citizen, but the relationship never was completely equal . . ." The point had been driven home to Polak when he served in the army. As a paramedic stationed in a Czech town, he made friends with some bookish Czechs in his unit: "Whenever I got high on some book and told my buddies they absolutely owed it to themselves to read it, they always wanted to know only one thing: 'Well, is this book in Czech, or is it in Slovak?' It never failed and it always stopped me dead in my tracks, because I didn't know! I had no idea! I'd usually have to go back and look at the book to find out what language it was in! And you know what? If the book was in Czech, then by all means, my Czech buddies were dying to read it, but if it was in Slovak — my God! Forget it . . ."

And so the bottom line of Slovak nationalism was a lack of respect — the Slovak separatists liked to point out that abroad, few people knew Slovaks even existed. The World According to Slovak Separatists knew of Czechs, or the imaginary Czechoslovaks, but it was rarely aware of the fact that there existed Slovakia, a lovely land of some five million people.

On the pie chart of the world population, the Slovaks amounted to one one-thousandth of the planet's people while the Czechs came in at two one-thousandths, so this whole Step-Aside-You're-Blocking-My-Sun Beef struck me as fairly petty — in Chicago, the entire Czechoslovakia with its Three One-Thousandths of Mankind rang very few bells, even back when Mike Ditka was still coaching the Chicago Bears and calling himself a "dumb Polack" in press conferences. When the sports writers pointed out to him that he was in fact of a Ukrainian-Slovak heritage, Ditka popped his chewing gum and Summed It All Up — "Same difference . . ." he said.

NEW POLITICIAN OF THE EAST

The person driving the break-up of Czechoslovakia was the Slovak leader Vladimír Mečiar, who could have made a swell Teamster boss — with his low forehead, the square jaw, the big gut, the thick hair that held its color wonderfully, and the blue-collar manner, Mečiar was cut out of the same cloth as Yeltsin, Walesa, and the other New Politicians of the East, even though he was a lawyer by trade. He had once been a boxer and, in politics, he remained a counterpuncher, but his appearance belied a quick wit and a splendid memory.

Mečiar, however, also had a Dubious Enigmatic Past: he had been accused of being an agent of the Soviet KGB by an old *STB* spook — there was an investigation by Prague, countercharges, files disappearing, more charges, and, finally, the *STB* accuser fleeing to Switzerland in fear of his life.

It was never established whether Mečiar had indeed been a KGB spook or not — the investigation expired when Czechoslovakia broke up and Prague lost jurisdiction over the case — but in the strange politics of post-Communist Eastern Europe, was it too far-fetched to imagine that Mečiar had split the country in order to kill the investigation and save his political skin?

DAPPER DRESSER

"When Mečiar lowered his shoulder and took off to ram down the door of Slovak independence," went a Prague joke, "Klaus had merely sprung it wide open for him . . ."

The Czech politician assisting Mečiar in breaking up the country was a dapper dresser with salt-and-pepper hair. Václav Klaus played tennis and basketball and he was so slim that, in the Beer-and-Glorious-Grease Czechoslovakia, he looked almost sickly. Even though Klaus had always been a strict monetarist at heart, he'd had a cushy job at the Economic Forecasting Institute under the Communists and had always behaved very cautiously toward the dissidents.

"I remember the day Havel brought Klaus to the Laterna Magica," Joska Skalník told me, referring to the Long Days of the Short

Velvet Revolution when Havel's revolutionary council would meet in the underground theater near Wenceslas Square. "He just sat there and observed everything — you were still taking a chance back then and you could tell this guy certainly wasn't going to stick his neck out in any way, shape, or form . . ."

When it was safe to do so, however, Klaus showed his stuff and it was enough to get him the job of minister of finance in the first post-Communist government. And while President Havel kept musing about "apolitical politics" and bursting all the Pompous Pretensions of Presidential Decorum, Klaus put together an efficient party machine which, in June of 1992, won the Czech elections.

Shortly after he became the Czech prime minister, Klaus stepped back and looked at the country of Czechoslovakia with his economist eyes, evaluating its feasibility in a cost/benefit fashion. He concluded that the Thin-Skinned, Difficult, Rural Slovaks were costing his government too much money and energy, and sprung the Door of Independence wide open.

TAKE THE DAMN ALFA ROMEO OR I'LL DROP DEAD

In the fall of 1992, some Slovak Romanies were voting with their feet and moving from the future Slovak Republic to the Czech Republic. This migration infuriated the fringe Czech Republican Party, led by one Milan Sládek, a photogenic former Communist censor, who claimed the American Republican Party for his inspiration. Sládek's Czech Republicans had managed to grab fourteen of the two hundred seats in the Czech Parliament, mostly by calling for "the cleansing of the gypsies" from the Czech Republic, and now Sládek announced he would reward the municipality that would "do the most to get rid of its gypsy population" by donating an Alfa Romeo to its police department. He then pondered the migration stats and declared that the small town of Jirkov in Northern Bohemia had earned his Alfa Romeo.

The racist award greatly embarrassed the mayor of Jirkov and he categorically refused to take the car.

The mayor's decision, in turn, upset the town's cops who had looked forward to zooming around in the Alfa Romeo — the police staged a labor slow-down, but the mayor held firm.

Finally, a Republican Parliamentarian came to Jirkov to force the issue. He declared a hunger strike until death or until city hall took the Alfa Romeo — in Czech politics, even the most desperate last resort of protest could become a Take-The-Damn-Alfa-Romeo-Or-I'm-Dropping-Dead fit.

The Parliamentarian fasted for two weeks. He was nearing the point of irrevocably damaging his body when his fellow Republicans talked him into calling off the strike and returning to Parliament, for the center held and the mayor of Jirkov never budged.

ANATOMY OF A BACK-ROOM DEAL

The amazing part of the split of Czechoslovakia was that the whole thing had been a back-room deal by Klaus and Mečiar. Didn't the break-up of a viable country require at least a clear consent of its citizens? Didn't it take a referendum? Particularly since the politicians driving the issue hadn't even been elected by the majorities of their voters? Particularly since they hadn't campaigned for the separation, either?

I watched Klaus address the issue on television: in his standard Father-Knows-Best-And-Has-No-Time-to-Explain-It-To-The-Developing-Minds-Right-Now-But-One-Day-You'll-All-Understand manner, he flatly ruled out any referendums: the Czechs and Slovaks were so confused by the notion of the split, he said, that, purely for sentimental reasons, their majorities might even vote to keep Czechoslovakia together — "and then what do we do?" Klaus asked.

Say what?

The man reminded me of the New Jersey state senator who had once said: "To hell with the public! I am here to represent the People!" — Klaus was rising above principle and splitting the country period, and damn what the benighted, heart-driven body politic thought about it.

FAR SIDE OF TELEVISION

On television, Klaus exuded narcissism and arrogance, but the world looked much simpler on TV screens than it really was — in the spring of 1993, I ran into my old professor of physics, Milda Brandejský, and he told me an insider's story about the prime minister.

My old teacher from the *gymnasium* of the Provincial Town of Thirty Thousand Souls got so swept up into the Velvet Revolution that he had quit teaching and threw himself into politics. He wound up a high level official at the ministry of interior. His was a gruelling, around-the-clock job and he talked wistfully of chucking it one day and buying a distillery in the Bohemian Highlands, but this was probably just talk — he didn't seem burned out by the work at all. And when we had dinner together, he told me how he had recently met Klaus.

It happened in some restaurant where the winning party brass were getting acquainted with their leader. The party functionaries sat around large tables and the prime minister moved through the room, taking their suggestions and humoring their peeves. He had only worked half the room when he dropped on a chair across the table from Brandejský. As everyone in the group introduced himself, my old professor of physics mentioned he'd had Klaus's son in his class a few years back.

"And that was it for the party conference!" Brandejský described the scene. "Klaus brought his chair over to me and never budged from my side for the rest of the evening." The prime minister completely forgot about politics. "He gave me the third-degree on every little thing his son had done in my class," Brandejský reported. "I felt like I was flunking out because I couldn't remember enough details."

The hard-working politician was suddenly only a father and all he wanted to talk about was his boy. "He's a little slower, but boy, does he work hard! Doesn't he?" the prime minister gushed about a student that Brandejský could barely remember — his boy was mildly retarded, but Klaus loved him all the more dearly for that.

DO SOMETHING FOR YOUR COUNTRY

No referendum on the split of Czechoslovakia was ever held because, finally, no one in Prague really gave a damn.

"Yeah, this break-up is a pity in a way," a bakery manager told me, "because now soccer and hockey will never be the same . . . It's always a lot of fun when we play the Slovak teams in the first division. On the other hand, now we'll finally bury Belgium in beer-drinking."

He was talking about the Race in the Per Capita Consumption of Beer in which Czechoslovakia had been the perennial runner-up to Belgium — I remembered this bogeyman haunting the Czech collective unconscious from my childhood: I'd watched grown, beady-eyed men stagger around a flag-draped barrel of beer and exhort each other to Do Something for the Country: "Yo, men! Drink up! Come on, let's kick some Belgian butt! Bottoms up, everybody! One! Two! Three!" But with the wine-drinking Slovaks dragging the Czech stats down, it was never enough, and the Belgians always managed to keep ahead by a couple of liters a year till December 31, 1992.

In Prague that night, you barely noticed the demise of Czechoslovakia. In Bratislava, the capital of Slovakia, some thirty thousand youths danced in the streets. In Košice, the second largest city in Slovakia, and in most of the other towns and cities of the old Czechoslovakia, there was a Big Fat Dog-Died Silence, but on the Morava River another Short Nasty Little European Border went up — one year after Germany had reunited to the north, west, and south of Prague.

MANUFACTURE OF MAGIC MEMORIES

I thought the break-up of Czechoslovakia was a bad idea and I regretted it too, for I'd left some indelible memories on the far side of the Nasty Little European Border — back in my Czech life, in the summer of 1968, my Dad, my younger sister and I jetted to the capital of Slovakia for a soccer game. *Sparta Praha* was playing in Bratislava, a city of half a million people straddling the Danube

River, at a time when my father was still cooking the books of his factory branch of the national bank in the Provincial Town. His embezzlement had entered its final, reckless stage and he was drinking heavily, so money was no object.

I recall a city bathed in a shimmering summer light, recall the lipstick lips of the long-legged, lovesome lovelies of Bratislava promenading up and down the cool *corso* by the Danube River, recall them giggling and whispering and giving me the eye and wearing things I didn't even know how to name — I suppose now that these were leggings or ballet tights or turbans or pantaloons, or some other kind of metro clothing no one in our Provincial Town had ever been seen in. I recall the bright-colored posters announcing that Bill Haley and his Comets were coming to rock Bratislava around the clock — on that summer weekend in 1968, for the first time in my life, I entered the gravitational field of a Western metropolis: Vienna lay some forty-five car-time minutes away and, if I stopped thinking of the sexy chicks I'd seen on the *corso* long enough for the erection to subside, if I lay still on my back on the hotel bed and closed my eyes and turned myself into meditational jelly, if I switched my consciousness out of focus and let it ooze over the landscape, I could almost sense the pull of the Alluring Free Enigmatic Non-Communist World on the Far Side of the Blue Danube.

I don't recall anything from the soccer game at all. I'd gone to hundreds of Sparta matches with my Dad, and in my mind they blend into a gazpacho of great goals, spectacular fouls, blown penalties, unjust ejections, a couple of memorably broken legs, and a few bobbing stretchers — the only thing I still remember from the *Sparta Praha* vs. *Inter Bratislava* game was its half-time: I entered the crowded men's room and was standing by the shell when someone stepped up to the pissoir on my right. I took a quick side glance at him, because this wasn't a place where you looked around, and realized that we had a black-and-white photograph of this man in every classroom of our school, smiling sadly under a pane of glass, an abstract and ethereal being you couldn't even imagine going to the bathroom, but now here he was, Alexander Dubček the Yes-Yes-Comrade Soviet-Educated Game-Hunting Gentleman Communist and the Chairman of the Communist Party, the most powerful man in the country, pissing side by side with me, as if he were just another soccer fan who'd had a couple of beers.

And right there, for some reason, I thought of a story my old man had told me about his hero: Winston Churchill walks into the WC of the British Parliament, sees the Labor Whip by a shell near the door, and makes for the far corner of the room.

"Oh, come off it, Winston," the Labor Whip gets offended, "we may not see eye to eye politically, but it's a sad day for Britain if we can't even piss side by side anymore . . ."

"We certainly can't," Churchill doesn't miss a beat, "because whenever you socialists see anything big, you always want to nationalize it . . ."

That night we ate dinner in an opulent hotel, the same place where the Sparta players were staying, and Dad brought the Dashing Right Striker Jurkanin to our table. The old man had been drinking all afternoon, his pronunciation was fuzzy and his gestures were larger than life by then — I was crossing my fingers, because you never knew what Dad might do when he was feeling no pain like this, but that night he was on his best behavior. I recall how he ordered a beer for Jurkanin which the young man tried politely to decline — back then Jurkanin the Biggest Talent of Czech Soccer, the Incomparable Dribbler who had started to play in the Big Show at the age of sixteen, was still only seventeen or eighteen, just a couple of years older than I was, yet from the way he looked at the glass it was clear he really had a taste for that beer, and my Dad read Jurkanin's look too and insisted the young man keep the beer, but he did so very gently and light-heartedly, and the sudden delicacy of his social touch was very gratifying.

I recall how I sipped my orange juice and Jurkanin sipped his beer and he gave the eye to my sister — my blushing kid sister, tall for her thirteen years, who had lately been sprouting breasts. And I recall my Little Sister suddenly acting real cool and real grown-up, as if she were my Big Sister, while my Little Brother of a Father resumed fawning drunkenly over Jurkanin — life being what it was, Jurkanin would never fulfill his great promise; he would always be able to put his fab head fakes on a couple of defenders, but he'd keep dreaming of the third move, of a slalom through the entire defense, and that third dribble would keep eluding him, and he'd never develop the great striker's killer instinct by the net, so he'd play for the national team for a few years and then hang on with *Sparta Praha* for the rest of his career, fading a little every year and winding up a journeyman player . . .

It was only much later that I realized what our Grand Jet-Setting Weekend in Beautiful Bratislava had really been about — by that summer, no longer believing he would pull off his embezzlement, Dad was preparing everyone around him for the moment when his con was exposed. He figured he'd soon be arrested and put away for many years and, being a family man to the bitter end, was structuring our future memories of him — he wanted his picture to linger in our heads in the Soft-Focus Shimmering White Aura of Overlit Glamour, as he introduced Dashing National-Team Dribblers to us while a Strolling Gypsy Violinist Fiddled Away in the background, the Chairman of the Communist Party pissed in the men's room around the corner, and Money was No Object.

BOOK
OF THE
TRUE
SELF

THEORY OF ANOTHER SELF

What makes another self? A journey. Where? To the second self. What makes the second self true? The language of dreams. What makes the first self go on? Knowing it had once been true. What makes the first self true again? The journey back.

PINK BIKE AND SPINNING SHOPPING CART

By the spring of 1993, Sonja spoke flawless Czech and wrote the language in cursive — no one could tell her apart from the other first-graders in her class at the Jan Masaryk school in *Vinohrady*: why did I think that the adaptability of six-year-olds was scary? Wasn't this exactly what I'd wanted? Didn't I manage to check the Growth of the Unknown Within her? Or had I merely Squared the Unknown Within?

While Sonja's Czech blossomed, basic mistakes had begun to weed her English. She "taked back moves" in chess, she "drinked milk" with "other childrens," she formed odd tenses and crammed English words into Czech idioms — at home, it was easier for everybody in the family to speak Czech.

One afternoon, Sonja and I were buying yogurts at the corner grocery store when I was suddenly struck by the unwieldy, Second-World look of the selection in the dairy cooler. "Hey, do you remember the great yogurts we had at home?" I asked Sonja wistfully.

She stopped to think about it, then shrugged her shoulders: "No . . . Can I have some chewing gum, Dad?"

"You don't remember the American yogurts? The Yoplaits? In the little cups that are narrower at the top? You really went for the peach flavor, remember? Or you liked raspberry too . . ."

"I dunno . . ."

"But you do remember the supermarket, don't you? The big long store with millions of things in it?" I could see she was really searching her memory, but then she shook her head. "Oh, come on . . . Don't you remember how you'd always hop right on the front of the shopping cart and I'd spin you around?"

"Oh, yeah! Yeah! I remember!"

She still held on to the memory of spinning round and round on a shopping cart, but in her recollection the well-lit, open space behind the cash registers, the shiny linoleum, the long isles converging by the back wall had peeled off — she was spinning around in an abstract space, for Chicago had dimmed to a dark obstacle course in her mind: five-year-olds didn't retain much, I realized, and Sonja had now lived some thirty percent of her verbal life in Czech.

"And you gotta remember your little bike, too!"

"Oh, yeah! I remember my bike, Dad!" her face brightened up — she was up against my urgency and was happy to oblige me.

"And do you remember me running after you every day on the way to preschool? Remember how you didn't know how to jump off and I had to run with you and catch you on every corner?"

"Oh yeah! Dad!? Can we do that again?"

"Oh, sure."

"Where is my bike?"

"Well, it's in Chicago with the rest of our stuff. You know, all your little toys, your bunk bed, our furniture."

"Can I have that chewing gum now, Dad? Please?"

The furniture, the old toys meant nothing to her anymore — she had sustained her own hit on the head with a blunt instrument and couldn't imagine she had a small pink bicycle, a menagerie of stuffed animals, a shelf of books, a bag of Legos, and a box of crayons somewhere else. The Cold Tough Chicago of Hard Edges was a veil of mist, an illusion, a thing of vapor and dream in her mind, for she was too young to have a second self: kids could only handle one self, and Sonja's true self was Czech, her true reality was Prague, she was my little Czech girl now.

A FINE, A BET

We were coming back from a hockey game in a provincial city. Adam's Slavia had dominated the poorly coached boys of the small town and he was in high spirits, but everyone else was crabby: we had run into some bad construction traffic under Hradčany Castle and still had all of Prague to cross.

"Too bad we can't just leave the car here and get on the Metro," sighed my wife as we inched our way past the *Hradčanská* station of Prague's clean, fast, efficient underground.

The offhand remark got Adam all riled up: "Hey, you guys, how about I race you home on the Metro?! Please? I bet I can beat you there!"

He had the Metro down, and the streetcar routes too, for he had been traveling around the city on his own: the Czech fourth grade let out at twelve-thirty every day and his hockey practices didn't start till three thirty, so he'd usually find some reason to go downtown. He'd hop on the Metro to go and get some caps for his gun, or a milk shake at one of the four McDonalds, or he'd finance a quick trip to the amusement park in the *Letná* neighborhood for a couple of his buddies. He'd stop home briefly, then take a streetcar to the hockey ring — for a ten-year-old with some street smarts, Prague was a safe and thrilling city.

"Come on, Dad! Please?!"

"Young man, may I see your ticket?" I pretended to be a tough ticket inspector, for Prague's public transportation ran on a qualified honor system. It was up to the rider to buy a ticket and stamp it, or to get a monthly pass. There were no ticket takers, only a few plain-clothes inspectors roaming the underground. They helped the honest people stay honest by catching the "black riders" and fining them two hundred crowns, or about seven dollars.

"I don't have to pay yet, sir, I'm only nine and a half," Adam lied, quickly donning his role in the skit — he had in fact just turned ten, but he too now passed for a Czech kid easily. Children under ten years of age rode the public transportation for free, but they were not allowed to travel alone.

"Well, if you're not yet ten, young man, then where's your Mom or Dad?" said the inspector in me.

"Well, I'm almost ten already, sir. Just a couple of months," said Adam.

"I'm sorry," I said in my changed voice, "but if you're not ten, then we'll have to go and call your parents."

"It's okay, Dad!" Adam dropped out of the role. "Seriously! They never stop kids! I don't know even one kid they ever stopped. We just run right past them . . ."

"I'm sorry, young man!" I stayed in my inspector voice. "But you're coming with me! I've got a bug up my butt today . . ."

"Okay, fine! So I lied! I am ten! And I don't have a ticket! And I'll pay your stupid fine!" Adam shot back, suddenly being himself and the not himself at the same time.

"Oh yeah? Listen to him!" his mother said. "You'll pay the fine, huh, you pipsqueak?!"

"All right . . . You owe me two hundred crowns, young man!" I said.

Adam unbuttoned the breast pocket on his jean jacket. He reached in. He pulled out two shiny green hundred crown bills — he was prepared for every eventuality.

"I don't believe this," his mother said. "You've gotta be kidding me . . ."

"See? So can I go, please?" said Adam — we had passed the station and begun to pull away.

I looked at his mother. She shrugged her shoulders: "Well, he *is* out there riding practically every day . . ."

Adam tore out the back door: "Bet you ten crowns I'll beat you home!"

Everybody knew the Metro was much faster: he was betting on a sure thing. "You're on!" I said to spice it up for him. "No way in hell you can beat us!"

"Hurry up, Dad! Step on it!" Sonja immediately got into the spirit of the wager.

We watched Adam sprint back toward the sculpture garden above the Metro station. He was prancing like a colt, had his own keys, was Mr. Independence himself.

"I can just see him in Chicago, trying to sneak on the CTA to go downtown . . ." his mother sighed, "Boy, does he have a nasty surprise coming, the poor kid."

When we got home, Adam lay stretched out on the sofa, staring at the clock. "I've been here nine minutes already, you guys! Where's my ten crowns?"

"That's not fair!" yelled Sonja. "How come he's got so much money and I don't have anything! He already has the two hundred and now you're gonna give him more?!"

I gave each one of them a ten-crown bill, and Adam appeased his little sister by taking her on a candy run to the corner store — he had now lived ten percent of his life in Prague, his spirit was much larger for it, and I wanted him to enjoy the freedoms of a Czech childhood while it lasted. We only had another couple of months in the country and I'd soon have to clip his wings in Chicago.

FREAK OF LETTERS

I was doing more talking than writing in Prague — two of my books were quickly published there and the literary people saw me as an Odd-Ball Freak of Letters, the English-Writing Czech, so I was getting a lot of ink in the papers. And then I was on a popular talk show and had a long prime-time interview on television, for the Czech public longed to see itself through American eyes. (The world was short on curiosity and most people only wanted to know about themselves — my books straddled two cultures and the Americans almost always focused on what I wrote about America, the Czechs on what I had to say about them.)

With all the publicity came a social life that was massive by my hermit standards; people started to recognize me on the street; strangers called and stuttered on the phone; forgotten acquaintances wrote touching letters; and, finally, a stocky, middle-aged dame in a Huge Wheel-Of-Fortune Purple Hat began to stalk me — there was no way I could concentrate on writing, but a writer who wasn't working wasn't easy to live with.

My wife took up oil painting. Zdena had always had a good eye and a knack for drawing, working with her left hand even though she wrote with her right hand, but the small oil painting I remember the best from Prague was exceptionally crude — two figures on a checkerboard floor that reached half way up to a turquoise sky. The figure on the left was one-third larger, a tire of fat around the middle, dressed in a white T-shirt and blue pants, mostly against the swimming-pool sky, androgynous but probably female, with her arms raised up as if she were in a stickup, as if she were about to give up and float away, the body and the arms a sort of a balloon.

The smaller figure, also androgynous, but probably male, fully dressed, almost completely swallowed in the ordered checkers, was rushing toward the human balloon with a lot of energy, its arms extended as if to grab her, as if to hold the balloon down — the ugly couple caught up in a strange dance of escape and surrender, possessiveness and aggression, weight and size, checkerboard and sky, order and disorder: Prague was tough on our marriage, and when I looked at the little painting, I missed my Private, Boring, Mortgage-Stressed and Productive life in Chicago.

TRUE BLUE ROMANTIC

That small oil painting could have been an allegory on Czech Communism, for the post-Communist Communist party was in a war with itself. As soon as the revolution shoved the Communists to the margin of Czech politics, the people who had once owed their Cushy Chairs and Perks to the Dictatorship of the Proletariat quickly moved on to the new pork-barrel parties. A few pragmatic Communists tried to rename the party, merge with other left-wing groups, and make themselves look like the German Social Democrats. They even condemned the "excesses of the last, stagnant period of the totalitarian rule," but they were the false self of the party and they were bitterly opposed by the Over-My-Dead-Body-Communist True Blue

Romantics who loved the party name, adored its murderous past, and talked of splitting into Bolshevik cells and going underground to whisper passwords, organize strikes, make bombs, and sing songs.

The split in the Communist party came to a head over one Bohumil Štěpán. This party fat cat from the old days of totalitarian power had ordered the brutal beatings of student demonstrators, which caused the Putative Death of Martin Šmíd. He was sentenced to eighteen months for it, then expelled from the Communist party by the reformists. But in the fall of 1992, Štěpán was back: he had done his time, penned a memoir in prison, and now he was asking for his old Red Card.

Štěpán was clearly a political liability to the Gentle Clean New Communist party, so its politburo turned him down, but some rank-and-file romantics saw comrade Štěpán as a People's Martyr Who Had Suffered in a Fulsome Capitalist Prison For His Bolshevik Beliefs and a party cell in the working-class *Vysočany* district of Prague quickly announced it was welcoming Štěpán back.

The chain-smoking chairman of the *Vysočany* Communists lived in a dank Dickensian apartment with drawn shades. There was a life-sized portrait of Stalin and a huge library with the collected works of Marx, Engels, Lenin, and Stalin — the Ancient True-Self Comrade flew into a rage when he was asked how the new Communist Party leaders felt about his decision to bring comrade Štěpán back in from the cold: "I don't give a damn what they feel! Ain't no politburo gonna tell *Vysočany* who can join up here, and who can't! Not no more! Uh uh! They can kiss all that totalitarian shit good-bye!"

REALITY OF ANOTHER SELF

Over a breakfast, Adam was telling us about a dream he'd had — a tiger on the loose, a lot of people scurrying around, Adam hiding behind a park bench, sort of afraid but not really, more thrilled than anything else — and I saw my opening immediately: "Did these people speak Czech or English?"

"I dunno . . . They were just hollering."

"What about the people in your other dreams lately?" I pushed for a confirmation of my theories of the true self.

"Nobody ever talks in my dreams," he shrugged his shoulders, so I switched my attention to Sonja: "What about your dreams, baby?"

"I don't got any dreams, Dad," Sonja announced definitively.

Zdena looked at me and burst out laughing: "I just had a dream in German the other night!"

BOOK
OF A
FAMILY
HOTEL

FOREWORD

In Prague, I kept running into Czech émigrés who were returning to the old country for good. Often they were coming back from the fringes of American life, for few of the Czech exiles who had made a name for themselves in the First World of New York, London, or Paris — people like Miloš Forman, Martina Navrátilová, Milan Kundera, or Rafael Kubelík — were moving back to the Cozy Operatic Small-Pond Prague.

The émigrés who returned were coming back to help the old country, or to reclaim a part of themselves they had lost in the New World, or simply to take back old family property, and their stories sometimes had the scope and the richness of a fine historical novel — in the winter of 1992, in a city famous for its beer, two sons of the Ledecký family repossessed their old family hotel. They had returned to Plzeň after more than forty years in America to take over the Hotel Continental, and later I came to look into the American rebirth of an old Czech institution: driving to Plzeň I wondered, what was passed on when a family reclaimed its past? How did a family maintain its identity on a faraway continent? Who could reconnect to anything in the past after forty years? Could a way of life survive the brutal twists of Central European history in America?

FOUR PEOPLE WITH TWO NAMES

Plzeň was a tough city of two hundred thousand people in western Bohemia. It had a historical heart, but the old Plzeň was a Place Under Dusty Construction and the new Plzeň was the Issue of Communism — huge, polluting factories, unwashed trolley buses, gray tenements of prefab housing, and hideous culture houses. The main one, an aggressive pile of cracking cement and marble, was dubbed "the House of Horrors." And hovering over the city when I got there, like the stench of rotting sauerkraut, was the stink of pollution and backed-up sewers.

Booking my room at the American-managed Continental, I was struck by the contradiction between the interior of the hotel and its exterior: on the inside, the Continental was still furnished in the style of the Late Anemic Communism — the worn carpet in the hallway puffed up into a sad archipelago of little bubbles; ancient rotary phones buzzed in the grab-bag rooms; in the café, flimsy lily-bloom lamps shone on sepia drawings of small-breasted women, reclining in shyly erotic poses among sepia snails.

The splendor that was the Continental's more distant past showed in the stately, turreted exterior of the building and in its prime location — the hotel stood right off Plzeň's central square, overlooking a park. And once there had been damask, crystal, mahogany, custom-made fittings, fresh flowers, and discreet service; young men had run up and down the back stairwell with a tray of bricks, training for the job of a waiter; and the hotel's forty-six rooms had kept the staff of more than a hundred employees busy.

Back then, the Ledeckýs who owned the Continental were a family of four people with two given names: the big Emanuel and Eugenia were the parents of little Eugenia and little Emanuel. And everybody, including the wife's art-collecting parents, the Egerts, lived in the hotel.

When the war came and Germany took over Czechoslovakia, the head Gestapo man kept his Czech mistress in the hotel. She was a long-legged shop girl who "made scenes for him," Anna Kašpárková-Marešová remembered for me, looking back to the days when she had been the little Eugenia's live-in tutor, "she whined and begged him to stay with her every time his chubby wife came to visit from the Reich."

The Continental lived its life of petty scandals, small satisfactions, war news, and hopes until December 20, 1944 — toward the close of the Second World War, the Allies bombed Plzeň several times. They ruled the skies over Europe by then and Plzeň was an important industrial link in the German war effort. On the last day of school in 1944, the American bombers flew in to take out the town's main train station.

GROUND-ZERO, 1230 HOURS

Lída Hájková saw the American bomb, still unexploded, right as it was dropping through the hotel — it was a moment of utter clairvoyance, a Strange Perception of a Fatal Warp of Time.

Hájková was the bookkeeper of the Continental and she had been racing to close out her books when the air-raid sirens went off. Most of the other employees and guests were already hiding under the granite staircase in the basement shelter, which was believed to be one of the town's safest spots, but Hájková had taken too long counting the money. Suddenly, the first bombs started exploding by the train station. Just then her purse fell off the counter. She bent down for it, but "the thing was just sort of jumping away from me," she later described it. As she chased her handbag, Hájková heard a deafening blow behind her, so she turned and, over her shoulder, she saw Mr. Stolín the head waiter standing in the swinging door of the café kitchen and, right behind him, she caught her Glance of the Bomb, a flash of something ripping through the building, a big black thing sucked out of the sky by the astronomical force of gravity and crashing through the hotel and through her field of vision for a brief, infinitely expanding glimpse — and then Mr. Stolín wasn't there anymore and then, another blink later, she was seized by an inexorable force as, with ear-splitting noise, a thousand pounds of explosives detonated in the basement below her and she flew on the wave of air, hurling right out the back door of the kitchen into the courtyard behind it.

She was buried in debris, but she had been incredibly lucky: the jumping handbag, which had caused her to bend down and point her body at the door, saved her life. She suffered only a few scratches, and could go on to describe her Miraculous Perception of the Black Turd of Death falling through the hotel to claim one hundred and eleven lives.

BUTTERFLY STROKE

A moment earlier, in the twilight of the basement shelter, Anna Kašpárková had been shown the wristwatch by Dogan, a tall, dark Yugoslav lady killer in a German uniform, who was sitting on a chair beside her. "They'll start bombing at twelve-thirty, you watch," he'd told the pretty twenty-two-year-old.

"Get outta here," she said as the minute hand jerked and bombs started to rain down from the sky, "with a horrible whistling sound. It's terrible, really just awful, the noise," Anna Kašpárková-Marešová told me, "and you can almost hear it aiming for you."

She had just made several thoughtless decisions to put herself right under the dropping bomb — she had been Christmas shopping on the main square when the first air-raid sirens sounded and a young man had asked her to go to a nearby bomb shelter with him, but she declined. There followed a Progression of Road-Not-Taken Decisions before she found herself looking at the watch of this German soldier, this Dogan who was really a resistance spy — he had been tipping off Yugoslav partisans about all munitions shipments from Plzeň to the Balkans, and the Gestapo had already started to investigate him — waiting for the minute hand to jerk to the half-hour mark and for the fatal bomb to drop.

When the moment came, she jumped up with both her arms lifted over her head, as if she were a swimmer leaning into the butterfly stroke: "It's a direct hit!" she screamed as the unexploded, gravity-pulled, shrieking bomb came smashing through the wooden floors of the hotel, where Lída Hájková was still chasing her handbag, before it finally hit the metal grate on the kitchen floor and detonated. Anna Kašpárková was knocked down by the impact and the lower floors of the hotel caved in around her, though the outside shell of the building remained standing. In the rubble and the smoke, people were screaming and wailing and groaning and dying, and groping around with her left hand, Kašpárková felt the passports that Dogan carried in the folded sleeve of his shirt, the handsome Dogan, who lay somewhere right there under the rubble and moaned for help.

"They're coming, they're coming, they'll be here any minute . . ." she tried to comfort him, for she had she always been the kind of a woman who thought of other people before she thought about herself.

But weren't both her legs burned and full of shrapnel? Wasn't her right arm hanging down uselessly by her side? Wasn't a shattered bone sticking out of it? "I didn't feel pain . . ." she told me. "I was in shock." She only had the sensation of having the arm raised, of her right arm bearing into the butterfly stroke, and it would be weeks before she could put the right arm down in her mind, before she could correlate her idea of the permanently damaged limb with its real position.

In the months that followed, Kašpárková would be operated on several times, without anesthesia or painkillers, because she was deemed too young for the dangerous, habit-forming morphine. The wounds on her legs kept getting infected, the feeling in her shattered arm kept coming and going. She was finally released from the German hospital in March of 1945 and went home to her mother's house in Utušice — by then, the Americans flew over the country with impunity and, every day, the same fighter pilot roared in: "He must've known it around here," she said. He'd always come from the same direction, at mid-morning, and she'd always go out and stand by the garden gate and wave to him with her good arm and he'd wave back to her and then veer off toward Plzeň, to hunt down some German trucks or take out a train.

"He was here every day practically, for weeks," Kašpárková told me. And she was there for him too, for weeks on end, holding up her end of a very odd human connection, of which the war was full.

YOU POOR KID

A tragedy of this magnitude caused the survivors to spin Webs of Conjecture and Fatality around it — hadn't Emanuel Ledecký junior been stopped from putting himself under the falling bomb as surely as Anna Kašpárková was drawn under it? Didn't the boy's tutor, who would lose his life in the explosion along with Emanuel's father and grandfather, talk the eleven-year-old out of staying home from school that morning, even though little Emanuel had been slightly under the weather? Didn't the tutor convince the boy that the last day of school before Christmas was a dumb day to stay away from class, where nothing much would happen? And later, when the first warning sirens went off at noon, didn't Emanuel again try to sneak out of the school and rush home? Didn't destiny now employ his professor of Czech to intercept Emanuel in the door and order him down to the school air-raid shelter?

Only moments later, the bombs started falling. Safe in the school basement, Emanuel listened to the earth-shaking booms coming from the direction of the train station. When the bombers passed on, when the anti-aircraft artillery stopped firing and you heard only the screeching of sirens, school was let out for the day, the boys talking the usual tough talk of budding teenagers: "Man, too bad they didn't take out our damn school!" Emanuel hurried home, thinking he'd go right back out and hunt for shrapnel: most boys in Plzeň were avidly collecting American shrapnel — they loved everything American, because the Americans were defeating the hated Germans.

He crossed below the railroad tracks and, emerging from under the overpass, he was stopped by his first glimpse of the terrible destruction — shattered buildings burning, streets strewn with bricks, clouds of heavy dust swirling in the cold December air. As Emanuel stood there awe-stricken, a boy he knew stepped up to him to say: "If you think this is bad, you should see the Continental. They're just pulling the dead bodies out of there."

Emanuel took off, but before he could sprint all the way home he was halted by the Germans. Their Civil Defense had the whole street cordoned off: "Unexploded bombs! No one's allowed in!" But he had gotten close enough to see the hotel — and it was standing! (This surprising fact was later ascribed to the large windows and the large spaces inside the building — the café halls, the restaurant and the atrium permitted the energy of the detonation to disperse faster: a denser, more compact structure would have been leveled by the bomb.)

As the little Emanuel gazed at the hotel and hoped against hope that everything would still turn out okay, maybe, somehow, an old customer staggered out of the smoke. His face was black from the dirt, he had a torn hat on, he was coughing blood — he glanced at Emanuel and said: "You poor kid . . . I'm coming out of the Continental and I'm the only one who got out of there alive . . ."

And so the current of emotion switched yet again, sending the eleven-year-old kid to stagger around the German cordon and look desperately for some way to slip through, feeling all alone in the world. Suddenly, out of the swirling emotions, wind-whipped fumes, and all the human confusion, there emerged a woman Emanuel knew, an acquaintance of the family, and she said: "Your Mom and your sister are fine. They're in my house right now."

FATE OF THINGS AND DESTINY OF PERSONS IN WAR

The two Eugenias had narrowly missed their own dates with the bomb: the big Eugenia saved her life by going to a house on the outskirts of town where her own mother, Grandma Egert, lay sick. Grandma Egert was weaving in and out of consciousness: as it would turn out, she was dying — for the Ledecký family, this was a tragedy of Greek dimensions.

While hurrying to her mother, purely by accident, the big Eugenia had run into her daughter in the street. The sirens were blasting and little Eugenia had herself just been sent home from school, so she was racing for the air-raid shelter — she too would have been killed by the bomb if big Eugenia hadn't deflected her destiny.

As it worked out, both Eugenias wound up listening to the shattering explosions at the bedside of Grandma Egert, who had less than a day to live, and they watched the comatose old lady wave her arm repeatedly — as if she were ordering someone to come with her. "Grandma had always said that, when her time came, she was going to take Grandpa with her," big Eugenia told me, "and Grandpa Egert was killed by the bomb, so I guess that she did take him with her . . ."

In war, the fate of things was as strange as the destiny of persons. "Nearly everything in the hotel was destroyed by the bomb," Emanuel Ledecký remembered, "everything but the round glass lamp in my room . . ." He found the fragile globe of the lamp on the floor, miraculously undamaged: "The electric wire that it hung on must have given way only gradually, I don't know how else to explain it."

The hotel was in ruins, however. It had to close down and it would never quite recover its style again. And Emanuel spent the rest of the war in a man's coat, the sleeves rolled up, the hem pinned up artfully so that he wouldn't drag it on the ground.

At the end of April of 1945, before the Continental was repaired, a new batch of soldiers moved into it — they were the Americans who had taken the city of Plzeň, marking the easternmost point in their penetration of Czechoslovakia: Stalin would not let them liberate the nearby Prague, for he had already checked off the capital of the country on his empire list.

Neither Anna Kašpárková nor the Ledeckýs held their griefs against these Americans — "Why? They were only trying to help us."

SADNESS OF A DUTIFUL DAUGHTER

In 1931, Eugenia Egert was eighteen, a dark girl of great beauty, looking melancholy in the formal wedding photographs — she was a bride who cried on the way from church. Her parents had told her to marry Emanuel Ledecký, who was her senior by nine years, though he struck her as being so set in his ways he seemed "twice as old as me." Ledecký was a prematurely bald man of the world — he had done his apprenticeship in London and New York, where he had worked as a waiter at the Waldorf-Astoria. He was also a part-owner of a grand hotel which Eugenia's father coveted and which her dowry would purchase in full, and she was a dutiful daughter.

"I did as I was told, but I had to square it all away with my own heart," she said some sixty years later, giving me an explanation Maupassant would have appreciated, "I had to be the mistress of my own feelings."

Thirteen years into the arranged marriage, the Americans accidentally made Eugenia a beautiful widow, and, not long after that, they brought romance into her life. "One never knows how things will arrange themselves in life," she told me, "sometimes your fate falls into place just like the pieces of some mosaic . . ."

His name was John Heinz and he was one of the American lodgers in her bombed-out hotel. He was dark, deeply tanned from the long war campaign, and he had an Indian face sewn on the shoulder of his uniform. "Are you Indian?" Eugenia asked him when she first saw him, surprising herself — she hadn't thought she had enough English to string together a bare sentence.

"Sorry," he said. He was not an Indian, he was an army general. She knew that he was married in America, but wasn't the war over? Didn't the world ring with hope? Hadn't a splendid spring just clothed the town in blooming purple lilacs? Didn't she have a right to live her own novel?

The general was something of a romantic. He had found something in the beautiful widow that he could never have enough of, that he had to have forever. When he was ordered home, he told Mrs. Ledecký that he was just going home to get a divorce. He promised that he would be back for her as soon as he possibly could.

He seemed sincere, but other American soldiers were making See-Ya-Real-Soon-Baby speeches around Plzeň: Mrs. Ledecký didn't fully allow herself to believe him — this had been her war novel and it was ending and now she had the rest of her life, and the two children, and the huge hotel to take care of. She was giddily surprised when the general sent her a ring from America: the plot of her novel was taking a turn she hadn't dared to dream about.

The ring was a copy of the general's West Point insignia and it was brought by an intermediary — General Heinz was a man of influence. He knew the foreign minister of Czechoslovakia, one Jan Masaryk, and he had asked for his help in sending the ring to Plzeň. Masaryk delegated the matter to a young Czech diplomat in New

York. His name was Jiří Janeček and he had just been appointed to represent Czechoslovakia in the United Nations. Janeček brought the ring across the Atlantic on his next trip home, then asked his sister-in-law to deliver it to Plzeň for him — the young diplomat had no patience for improbable romances.

A few weeks later, purely by accident, the diplomat found himself in Plzeň. He was driving across the country with his brother and they happened to be low on gas. After the war, gasoline was a scarce commodity, sold only for special coupons. Staring at the gauge, Janeček remembered the lady hotelier he had just done a favor for — she might have a way of getting some black-market gasoline, he thought. He had his brother wait in the car outside the hotel while he went to see if the lady hotelier would return a favor.

The brother wound up sitting in the car for an hour. He was furious by the time the diplomat emerged from the hotel and, according to his son George, who would be conceived a few months later, told the brother right then and there: "I think I'm going to marry this lady."

"Janeček was a charming man, tall and rather handsome," Eugenia told me when I asked about her second courtship, "and then too, I could feel what was coming . . ." What was coming to Czechoslovakia was Communism, Nationalizations, Class Struggle, Hate, and Pettiness — "and I very much wanted to go to America with my children," said the big Eugenia, making it clear that the dutiful daughter had fully mastered her heart.

And so General John Heinz had taken too long to get his divorce. Beautiful Eugenia would keep his ring, but she would marry the diplomat who would take her, and her two teenage children, away from Plzeň, away from the painful memories, away from the coming brutality.

DIPLOMAT SHOPS FOR A HOUSE

The diplomat took Eugenia and her children to New York, where he became a career UN man, rising to the post of the Director of External Affairs, Office of Public Information. In America, Eugenia gave the diplomat a son and two daughters, and Jiří Janeček gave his two-tier family of seven a stylish life: "Every other year, the UN paid for our home leave," remembered George Janecek, the American-born son of Eugenia and the diplomat, "so we'd go to Europe on the big ocean liners. I sailed on all the *Queen Elizabeths*..."

But the diplomat didn't seem a man at peace with himself. The way his son remembered it, all his life, Jiří Janeček kept shopping for a big country house. The family would often go and look at impressive houses on the big lots of Westchester County, and the diplomat would talk to the realtors "as if money was no object," George Janecek told me, "but then he never put any money down..."

MISTRESS OF HER HEART

For some forty years, Plzeň held nothing but painful memories for Eugenia — back in 1948, as the rudeness and hatred that Eugenia had sensed coming since the end of the war arrived in Czechoslovakia, the Hotel Continental was taken away from the family.

Eugenia and her children were in New York by then, but Mr. Ulč, the old managing director whom Eugenia had left in charge, tried to save what he could. He argued with the new Communist managers that the nationalization decrees didn't cover the personal belongings of the Ledeckýs. His legal reasoning was sound. He was demoted. He watched helplessly as the best furniture, glass, dishes, and carpets disappeared from the Ledecký apartment. He looked on while the Egerts' collection of paintings was confiscated. He wrote guilt-ridden letters to Eugenia.

"No one could have possibly done anything about any of that. His efforts were downright heroic, but he took it all so personally," she told me, "and I think his marriage was rather unhappy too" — one day in the early fifties, the former director had had enough: he threw himself off the roof of the Hotel Esplanade in Marienbad where he had just been transferred.

For the next forty years, a string of Communist directors ran the Continental without pity. They paved over its garden restaurant with asphalt and made a parking lot. They stripped all the beautiful things from its interior and filled it with flimsy and tasteless furnishings. They threw up a lot of walls inside the luxurious rooms, cutting them up into a Warren of Narrow, High-Ceilinged Spaces — but Communism spent itself in a couple of generations, and, in 1992, the Continental was returned to Eugenia by the new Czech government. She was in her eighties now, too old to take charge of it, and she lived near her grandchildren in America, so she had a tough decision to make: who in the family should get the hotel that had made her a weeping bride?

At the time, her three daughters had families in America, but her sons, Emanuel from her first marriage and George from the second, were single. They had both gone to live in the Czech Republic, taking Czech citizenships, which only made Eugenia's decision more difficult, but she had never shirked a tough choice, even when it threatened to tear her two-tier family apart.

"My decision actually wasn't all that hard," she told me. Was it because her older son Emanuel had grown up in the hotel? Because he had fine Czech? Didn't her younger son George only speak broken Czech? Weren't the impressions of a few summer visits all George knew of the country?

Eugenia put George the American from Salt Lake City in charge of the Continental — "George is much more of a businessman than Emanuel, you see," she explained the paradox to me. "That's what George did all his life. Emanuel has no feeling for business. It doesn't interest him."

She was serene in her conviction, ever the mistress of her heart.

AN AMERICAN ABROAD

The American who came from Salt Lake City to reclaim the Ledecký hotel for the family was a handsome man in his late forties, healthily bald, fastidiously groomed, and outgoing. George Janecek had the You're-Right You're-Right Manner of a salesman, cracking jokes and talking about his life with an agreeable openness.

"I've lived in resort towns all my life, " he Summed Up His Past. "Provincetown, Aspen . . ." He had made his living there by custom-making jewelry: "I sold some belt-buckles for twelve hundred dollars. I had sports cars . . . Girlfriends . . ." But it was a dissipated life and, in his thirties, feeling adrift, Janecek decided to become a photographer. He made a living of that, too, till he saw his opportunity in Czechoslovakia — but the hotel he took over in Plzeň was shabby and its employees, corrupted by Communism, had grown used to ripping off the customers and the management. And Janecek didn't know the hotel business, or the family tradition, or the country.

"You know, George is a nice guy and all, but sometimes he talks so strange he might as well be a Martian," I was told at the Continental, where the staff had sized up their American boss a long time ago.

His employees were referring to Janecek's funny Czech, his manner of grating familiarity, his sales incentives ("just pidley crap compared to what you can make on the side" — by stealing), his incomprehensible staff meetings ("somebody should tell him Plzeň ain't America"), his ideas on management ("he talks about teamwork like the owner was just another player on the team") — in the eyes of the post-Communist opportunists on his payroll, George Janecek was just a Faintly Ridiculous Man.

And when he spoke of his hotel to strangers, Janecek talked about the Continental as if it were a fine, Western hotel — his idea of the place was so removed from its sleazy reality I kept remembering his father the diplomat and wondering: wasn't this American from Salt Lake City, in some sense, also trying to put down the money for the big country house of an important man? But could a man coming from America do so in Plzeň? With money he hadn't earned? In a place where money was soft and not particularly respected?

·

MEMORY FAILS THE GENERAL

In Plzeň I found out that the brightest memories of the Continental Hotel now belonged to an elderly gentleman who was living in Prague — when I met Emanuel Ledecký junior at a sidewalk café in the Old Town, he was wearing an unkempt musketeer moustache and clutching a bulky leather bag. It held a neat folder with the mementoes of his life and, stacked on top of it, four plastic bottles —

punctured with holes, they were slithering with snakes, four different species from three different continents.

"I'm a herpetologist," he explained, shyly, even while he enjoyed
the Oh-My-God What's-Next commotion his snakes caused in the
café.

The kid who had been so powerfully drawn by the bomb, and
then missed by it, seemed to have lived the rest of his life with the
echo of its detonation ringing in his ears: he told me how, ever since
he could remember, he had been attracted to the natural world, and
how his naturalist passion had saved him — he was never more in-
volved with nature than in the late forties, when suddenly he found
himself in rough New York, an adolescent living under a diplomat
stepfather who was keeping his mother occupied with new babies,
lost, grieving for his Dad and his beloved grandparents.

Fifty years later, Emanuel the herpetologist still found it painful
to talk about their tragic deaths in 1944 — his eyes welled up with
tears, for he was a sweet man. And though he had managed to parlay
his way of escaping from people into real accomplishments (he had
been a curator at the Boston Aquarium and at the Shedd Aquarium
of Chicago), he gave the impression that, unlike his mother and his
half-brother maybe, he wasn't fully the master of his heart.

It was only later, when I thought about how differently grounded
the half-brothers were (how Emanuel the dreamer who could seem
so eccentric in the details of his life had a more solid purchase on
reality than George the promoter who fancied himself tough and
clever in dealing with its details, but lived an illusion) that I was
startled by an idea: Didn't I know this man? Back in the early seventies? In Chicago? Wasn't he the guy with the snake stories who showed
up at all the Czech dancing balls? Didn't I use to see Emanuel Ledecký
regularly back then?

An émigré's world is small and fluid, and it throws up odd connections — Emanuel had once gone dancing with my sisters and my
future wife. He was pushing forty then. He was balding. He seemed
ancient to us. He came and asked our teenage girls for a dance, and
they waltzed with him, lifting their eyes to the ceiling — he wasn't a
bad dancer, but he spoke an accented Czech and tried too hard to
amuse them with stories about boa constrictors escaping from his

house and slithering down fire escapes, or poisonous snakes he had smuggled into the country under his shirt, or toads suddenly hopping out of socks and across crowded laundromats — they were true stories, entertaining and strange, but Emanuel Ledecký wasn't very assured of himself and he was too old and too kind, and we laughed at him.

Was this sweetness what big Eugenia saw in the man when she looked at Emanuel? Was that why she had decided to deed the family hotel to his younger brother, the American abroad, even though Emanuel was clearly better suited to become the keeper of the family tradition? And yet, did it matter how Eugenia ranked her sons? Did it make any difference who got the hotel, finally? Were the family traditions made on beds, turrets, and switchboards? Or were they made on ideas, memories, and feelings?

The Ledecký past didn't come along with the building in Plzeň, and it was clearly up to Emanuel now to keep the most moving chapters of the History Book That Was the Hotel Continental. And Emanuel had been working on it, contemplating the might-have-beens of the family past and examining its faulty connections — cradling the snakes on his lap in Prague, he told me how, in the eighties, when he was much older than John Heinz had been at the end of the war, he visited the American general who had fallen so madly in love with his mother. "I was just passing through this town in Florida where Heinz lived, so I decided to drop in on him . . . Why not?" he asked as if this were what everyone would have done.

The general was ninety two years old, still fit, still carrying himself like an old soldier. He had remarried after his divorce, and "his new wife was this very nice, white-haired lady. She clearly loved him and took wonderful care of him." John Heinz proudly showed Ledecký the photographs of his son, who had also become a career military man. They talked for an hour or two in the general's house, overlooking a lake. The new wife had earlier warned Emanuel that the general's memory was failing, but he had to ask anyway: "General, do you still remember my mother? Eugenia?" And the Hotel Continental? Plzeň? Your ring? Right after the war? And me? How close you came to becoming my stepfather?

The general took a long pause, and then he shook his head — no, he didn't remember Eugenia, he didn't remember the bomb-shattered, ghost-ridden hotel, didn't remember the ring, but even while he was denying everything, Emanuel was watching the old man very closely, and he didn't believe memory was failing the general so spectacularly — "something in the way Heinz said it made me wonder if he was telling the truth . . ." Emanuel told me in Prague. "The old soldier had been so happy to see me earlier . . . And then too, you've also got to keep in mind that his new wife was sitting right there" — the white-haired lady had to be in her late sixties or seventies, wouldn't she have known everything about the general's fatal romance in the bombed-out hotel? But could Eugenia still be a threat to her? Could it be that these insecurities never stopped gnawing? — "and she didn't budge from Heinz's side for as long as I was there . . ."

And so Emanuel Ledecky gradually realized that he would never be allowed to probe more deeply into the general's failing memory and that he was not going to procure another elegant regret about a turn his life might have taken, and he got up and said good-bye and, for a long beat, for the last time, he held onto the old man's shaking hand.

BOOK
OF
NEW
LANDS

CONQUISTADOR HEART

Many old hotels in Europe were printing new stationary, for if the street name hadn't changed on them, often the country name no longer applied — Slovakia was only the last of the New Émigré-Making Brain-Hemorrhaging Lands in the Old Communist East. You needed a score card to keep up with the places seceding and declaring independence from other territories, which themselves had only recently got their own thick line on the map.

The smaller the new lands got, the more dreamy they seemed. They had dreamy names like Moldova (from which the republic of Dnieper-Dniester was fighting to secede), or Tadzhikistan, or Naghorno-Kharabakh, or Abkhazia; they didn't print their own money or stamps; they often didn't even man their borders or control their territories — they were there to be taken by Seven Conquistadors in a Used Toyota Pickup Truck Mounted with a Howitzer. Often little more than temporary paper dreams of ambitious local politicians, the New Lands of the East made the conquistador heart of my son Adam leap up.

In the summer of 1990, as a family in a rented Volkswagen, we had made an attempt to go around the Black Sea. We were ultimately stopped from circumventing the sea by an outbreak of cholera in Romania and the lack of gasoline in the Soviet Union, but the journey made a geography buff out of Adam — he started collecting the countries he'd seen the way hunters amassed horns. He began his collection with ten items: Germany, Czechoslovakia, Austria, Hungary, Yugoslavia, Bulgaria, Turkey, Greece, and the Soviet Union.

A year later, the war in Yugoslavia broke out — we had driven down the Highway of Unity that stretched from Zagreb past Belgrade to Macedonia, so Adam added Slovenia, Croatia, Serbia, Bosnia-Hercegovina, and Macedonia to his list. Then the Soviet Union began to fall apart and, gradually, he put down Russia, Georgia, Abkhazia, and Armenia. Finally, one night while he slept calmly in his bed, Czechoslovakia expired and now he could count Slovakia too.

"You know something, Dad," he once lifted his eyes at me from the huge atlas which completely covered his legs and which he kept poring over, "Now I've been to eighteen countries . . . Can you believe it?"

"How about that? And most of 'em didn't even give you diarrhea, huh?"

"No, I didn't even have to put my shoes on! That's what I mean . . . Do you think I can like . . . Like really count 'em all though?"

LEPROSY, BANDITS, AND
CANNIBALS — A FLASHBACK

Our journey around the Black Sea came a couple of years before we moved to Prague. Right after the Velvet Revolution my Czech book was published there and the soft currency advance was large enough to buy the family a beach vacation on the golden sands of the Bulgarian coast of the Black Sea. Our itinerary snowballed from there.

In July of 1990, in a rented Volkswagen Golf, we set off from Prague, ignoring a Storm of Dire Head-Holding Oh-Boy Oh-Boy warnings. Our Czech friends and relatives begged us not to go to Bulgaria: there was not a drop of gasoline there, they said, a massacre of the remaining Turks was about to ignite a civil war, and the Black Sea coast was rife with cholera and hepatitis. And we'd be crazy even to think about driving through Romania, they said — Romania made Bulgaria look like a paradise. And of course the only place that could make Romania look good, they said, was Yugoslavia.

We drove straight across Yugoslavia, down Marshall Tito's Highway of Unity, then spent a fine week in the old Bulgarian port of Nesebur.

When we were leaving for Istanbul, our affectionate Bulgarian landlady and her family accused us of being terribly irresponsible: no one had the right to take two small children into Turkey — there was leprosy, bandits, and cannibals.

The Turks, it turned out, were a self-confident, playful, and honorable people. In the misty, tea-growing hills on the Black Sea coast, where the drying hazel nuts were piled up ankle-deep on every flat surface — on soccer fields, parking lots, and roofs — our Volkswagen got stuck in the mud of a road twisting toward an ancient thermal spring. The troop of swarthy construction workers who pulled us out were appalled to hear we were headed for the Soviet Union. This was child abuse as far they were concerned: there was no gasoline in the Soviet Union, no food, just government blackmail, rogue armies, and atheists — the Soviet Union was Death Black, Red, and White, With No Afterlife.

The Late Soviet Union did prove a land of puzzling paradoxes — all the gas stations were shut down, yet the streets were jammed with traffic; there were no cigarettes, yet everybody smoked; all the stores had empty shelves, yet every time we were invited into a house, a Damn-It-Forgot-The-Peacock-Feather-Again feast erupted in the dining room . . .

The paradoxes of Soviet life forced us to abandon our original ambition. It was impossible to go all the way around the Black Sea, so we decided to make a different loop and drive around the Caucasus — immediately, in Sukhumi, which would soon become the capital of Abkhazia, we were sternly warned not to risk going to Tbilisi, Georgia.

In Tbilisi, the Soviet Intourist officially ordered us to stay away from Yerevan, Armenia, where there was hunger and cold, not a drop of gasoline, Azeri saboteurs striking behind-the-lines blows in their war with Armenians, and opportunistic bandits at every switchback of the mountain roads.

We took the long way from Tbilisi to Yerevan, driving right around the war. The Armenian high plateau seemed an unending scroll of sandpaper, dotted only by tiny drops of orange as, here and there at the roadside, old women sold bunches of spectacular carrots. I coasted down the long hillsides to save gas and we made it to Yerevan and, finally, under the Shining White Kite of Turk-Held Mount Ararat Floating in the Cobalt Sky, reached the Terminus of All the Dire Warnings.

"I'd go with you in a minute," a receptionist in our Yerevan hotel sighed when we were checking out.

"But you don't even know where we're going . . ." I said.

"You're not going to Moscow, you're not going to Baku," she shrugged her shoulders, "everywhere else, it's better."

FACTS AND PATHOS, BABY

It was in the logic of the post-Communist world, where so many people lived in fear of the unknown and in fear of the other, that local wars erupted with regularity. Some were fought viciously, some half-heartedly, but most combatants understood that, in the modern warfare, a picture was worth a thousand bullets, a great picture a thousand hand grenades.

In the fall of 1992, Antonín Kratochvíl the Czech-born photographer from New York showed up in Prague with a magazine assignment. "Yo, baby!" he called me up, "we're gonna go to Croatia and we're gonna do the kids of the refugees, okay? I need you to pen about a thousand words, okay? Quietly moving, okay? Facts and pathos, baby, okay?"

Antonín was a big guy — not very tall, but massive, wide of shoulders, thick of belly, big of bone. Even his blond, curly hair had girth and had to be tied into a fat pony tail. But he had also once shot fashion for *Vogue* and knew how to wear flamboyant hats, scarves, snakeskin boots, and jackets, and he flowed through the world with a Cadillac strut — to stroll down the street with Kratochvíl was to become invisible: the eyes of all the pedestrians, all the drivers, all the passengers in the passing street cars immediately locked on Mod Sashaying Big-Boy Kratochvíl with Red-Food-Stains on his Snow-White Trousers and the faces lit up with smiles.

Kratochvíl loved the attention — it took me a while to realize that he had quite consciously reinvented himself: I had to watch Kratochvíl work in the refugee camps of Croatia to understand how his

Striking Flamboyant Dare-You-To-Look-Away persona was in fact an extremely subtle tool of his trade.

SENSITIVE MERCENARY

Antonín Kratochvíl's father had once owned a portrait studio in Prague. In the class-struggle cold-war Stalinist fifties, this made him an exploiter of the proletariat — his son wasn't even allowed go to high school: Antonín played hockey with some of the best juniors in the country, dabbled in smuggling suede to Poland, and, with the rest of the city's Golden Youths, Film Stars, Money Changers, and Fashionable Bohemians, hung out at the *Filmový Klub* in the center of Prague.

It was in the men's room of the *Filmový Klub* that another Golden Youth sketched a crude map for Kratochvíl on a soggy napkin — this young man had just broken his leg in the mountains on the border of Yugoslavia and Austria, while trying to defect with some other habitués of the bar. He couldn't move and was caught, but all his buddies had made it to the Glamorous West, and Kratochvíl was resolved to give it a shot too: "Back then, it was *the* thing to do . . . Just about everybody I knew split from the country."

The year was 1967. Kratochvíl made it to Austria, where the Glamorous West had a bunk bed for him in a dormitory of the refugee camp in Traiskirchen. "That joint stank like a railroad john and it was gangs of Czechs against gangs of Hungarians, or Albanians, or Yugoslavs . . . I slept with a heavy lock in my hand for six months there . . ."

He was nineteen years old and dreamed of going to America, but no overseas country wanted an unskilled immigrant. "Only Sweden would accept me. They took all of us *lager* rejects, as a humanitarian gesture. Me, I was supposed to be a beach guard in a hotel there, but the summer lasted one afternoon in Sweden . . . When that sun set, they expected the beach guard to save the dirty pots and pans in the kitchen."

Kratochvíl lit out for the nearest big city. Half a year later, he was still jobless, but renting a huge villa in the center of Malmö — he'd quickly found a way to make himself useful on the hashish smuggling trail between Denmark and Sweden, and briefly life was grand, too grand to last in fact: the next summer that flashed through Sweden saw Kratochvíl sewing postal bags in a local prison.

"So they're just bringing me to the slammer, I still got the handcuffs on and everything, and I hear somebody yelling: 'Antonín!' And I look, and I see this bunch of guys I knew from the refugee camps there! They were all doing time for robberies and stuff, and they're like: 'Cool, man! Now everything's finally falling into place! Now we've finally got us a real left wing!'"

The jail had a kick-ass soccer team, and Kratochvíl immediately became a speedy starter on it ("I was still a walking X-ray back then"). The prison squad had all the time in the world to practice, their games were all home games, and they had a scary bunch of fans — the team was about to clinch their division when Kratochvíl got word that he'd soon be shipped back to Austria. He had been scoring a lot of goals though, and his teammates were upset. They wanted Antonín "to punch a jail guard, so I could finish off the season with them! Unbelievable! I told them to kiss off . . ."

He found himself back in Traiskirchen, but now he was an ex-con and the Austrians wouldn't have anything to do with him. He was turned away from the camp. He had no documents and nowhere else to go. For a few weeks, he slept by the *lager* wall. It was fall and the days were getting shorter and shorter, and Antonín had to do something — "I finally decided to try to make it back to my buddies in Denmark, but I didn't want to risk crossing Germany. I thought maybe I could hop on a ship in Marseilles and go to Copenhagen that way, or something . . ."

He easily walked from Austria to Italy, then swam across the Riviéra border into France, but his luck ran out in the town of Menton. He was picked up by the French police. He gave them a different name, because he didn't want them to dredge up his hashish past in Sweden. "They just locked me up anyway and kept telling me they'd soon send me back home, back to the Commies . . . And then this real friendly Serbian guy starts hanging around and giving me cigarettes, Cokes, sandwiches . . . I didn't know what the deal was."

The friendly Serbian was no gay suitor, however — he was the recruiter of the *Légion Etrangère*. Kratochvíl resisted his pitch for a week, then signed on the dotted line — "so then they bring in this guy who speaks perfect Czech to debrief me . . ." The interrogator knew that Kratochvíl's story was full of holes, but didn't press the issue too hard. "I think more than anything else his job was to test me, to check out if I could take it . . ."

He proved legionnaire material and was flown to a boot camp in Corsica — "a real rough place: no sleep, someone in your face all the time, live ammo . . . They want to break you, to take you apart, and then put you back together as a machine for following orders." To graduate from the boot camp, you were supposed to attach a magnetic mine to the chassis of a tank rolling at you — "you were in this terrain full of holes and depressions and these tanks were hunting you down." You had to find a deep enough spot to let the tank roar right over you while you stuck the mine to its belly. "Some guys panicked, didn't pick out a big enough hole, and wound up splattered all over the panzers . . ."

Kratochvíl slipped his graduation mine on the tank and found himself in the Tibesti Mountains of northern Chad, fighting Marxist guerrillas. He was the gunner on search-and-destroy missions in the desert full of scorpions and snakes. He sat in the back seat of a jeep, wielding a machine gun, with the driver and a tracker in front of him. "We had good intelligence, plane reconnaissance, native trackers . . . It was pretty shitty out there in the mountains. Can't even remember it really . . . I spoke fluent French too, and now I can't speak it anymore, so I think I blocked a lot of it out . . . But anyway, the other side, they had their mines . . ."

Half a year into the five-year term of service, Kratochvíl's jeep ran over a mine. "All I can recall is the blast. CABOOM! When I woke up, I was on morphine . . ." The other two men in the jeep had died on the spot, but Kratochvíl lived with a Coke-can chunk of shrapnel in his belly: "The Foreign Legion has some of the best doctors in the world, you know . . ." Still, his wound kept getting infected in Africa and he was finally ordered back to France for recuperation.

In the Foreign Legion fort in the harbor of Marseilles ("they're just crazy about their forts, the French"), Antonín decided he wasn't going back to the Sahara period. He waited till his wounds were almost completely healed, then made a run for the rest of his life: "By deserting, I was risking a couple of years in a French military prison where they just about finished you off, but in my mind I pretty much had no choice."

He scaled down from the fort window on a rope, stole a sweater from some workers in the harbor he'd been casing for days, and snuck aboard a Paris train. His head was shaven. He wore hospital slippers. He had zero money and only a couple of hours to work with before he'd be reported missing.

On the Marseilles-Paris train, he chose a compartment holding a young woman and a beatnik type and started to work on his excuses for the conductor — "all of them inane." He was getting a big break, because the conductor didn't show up for the longest time. "We'd got past Avignon when he came. By then I figured the word that I was missing might have gone out to the railroads . . ." Now came the shock — the beatnik didn't have a train ticket, either. "I just couldn't believe this jerk!" This meant Kratochvíl didn't have a prayer with his excuses — for a moment, he thought he was finished, but right then his Guardian Angel came through big time. "Suddenly, out of the blue, this girl pulls out her wallet and she buys tickets for both of us! It was an awesome moment! She was in childbirth and didn't even know it! She was definitely giving me life, though." They hadn't exchanged as much as a look before then. He never saw her again. "She never knew she had saved me and all I know about her is that she was Norwegian."

He hopped off the train before it pulled into Paris, hitchhiked around the city, slept in cemeteries, crossed the border into Belgium, made it across that small country, and ran out of steam in Amsterdam: "Got a whiff of that beautiful liberal atmosphere there and walked into a police station and gave myself up. This time I gave them my real name . . . Said I'd just defected from Czechoslovakia and hitch-hiked straight to Holland."

The Dutch immigration people knew Kratochvíl's story didn't add up, yet they didn't press him. "I think that Dutch guy I was talking to could feel the depths of my desperation. I was pretty much a walking time bomb."

He was put up in a refugee hotel in Amsterdam, "where I slowly pulled myself together. At first, I was somewhere else completely: I slept fully dressed. I still fought in the Sahara in my dreams. Every night I was yelling and jumping out of bed to gun somebody down before they got me. Everybody in the hotel was scared shitless of me . . ."

And so Kratochvíl had been given one last chance to redeem his life, but he had no skills, no compass, no confidence that things could ever work out for him — when a Dutch social worker asked him what, if anything, he wanted to do with the rest of his life, "nothing exactly leaped into my mind . . . I finally said: 'I dunno, photography maybe?' only because that was what my old man had done."

But he passed the talent exams at the university with flying colors — he had soaked up his Dad's vocation at home and didn't even know it. "I was in hog heaven in that photography school . . . I was really bummed out every time they shut it down for the holidays."

In Amsterdam, he met Lorri, a young California girl, who would one day become the photography editor at *Rolling Stone,* and she took him to Los Angeles. "Talk about culture shock . . . All of a sudden, I'm balancing on a surfboard and eating dinners with a warm, loving family every night. I didn't know what the hell had hit me . . ."

IFFY LIFE FLEETING

Kratochvíl made money in America by shooting fashion for *Vogue,* nudes for *Playboy,* landscapes for *Condé Nast's Traveler,* portraits for *Première,* but his heart was in black-and-white reportage. He was drawn to extreme situations, and brought back images of people you almost couldn't bear to look at, such as the heart-breaking child cripples of the Afghanistan war, or pictures of those you couldn't very well openly stare at, such as gun-toting teenagers of Beirut, German skinheads, criminals, mental patients, junkies, hookers . . . Yet, he was working with a 28 millimeter lens, a very wide-angled glass, which forced you to get right into the thick of the action you were portraying.

"I like pictures where you can smell the stink of the armpits, you know," he joked about his aesthetic, but he also had the scars to show for all the times his cameras had been shoved into his face. "Working with a wide lens is a challenge and it's an adventure . . . The challenge is to blend into the situation, to make people forget about you and the camera. The adventure is that you never know when somebody may walk into the composition, or when your shadow may fall in it, or when something might happen that you're only seeing out of the corner of your eye and maybe won't even fully know about till you scrutinize the pictures at home . . . With a wide lens, you stay open to the world and yet you can take a very intimate reading of the situation."

Some of Kratochvíl's strongest images presented a kind of a fleeting glance: they were blurry with movement, or framed so that the bodies were cut off — you never had the full picture. There was a disturbing sense of things happening just outside your view, of a world in motion, a fluidity, a sense of threat. It was as if you only had a brief moment to orient yourself in an unfamiliar, complex situation; as if you were constantly scrambling and groping and hanging on for dear life; as if you never knew enough to have full confidence in your decisions; as if you always ended up reacting instinctively.

This photographer knew in the marrow of his bones how iffy and odd life could be, and his images were awash with the strangeness of human existence — wasn't the camera just transporting Kratochvíl back to the pounding-heart moments of his incredible biography? Wasn't he in some way using his Nikon to prove himself over and over again on some foreign-legion tank grounds? Wasn't he roaming the war zones, slums, and mean streets of the world with his camera merely to recapture the bruising rush of feeling and perception you felt driving through the booby-trapped mountains of the Sahara? But could a man who'd once hunted human beings with a machine gun ever express his sense of what life was using only the nuances of light? How did you get beyond coming to your senses on morphine, with your belly ripped open by shrapnel? How the hell could Kratochvíl ever shoot fashion after that anyway? But wasn't doing whatever you had to do to survive the whole point of his scattered, violent life?

NAP UNDER A BLOOMING LINDEN TREE

Kratochvíl's assignment took us to a refugee camp, called Gašinci. It lay in the easternmost tip of the Crescent-Shaped Soft-Bordered Croatia, some twenty miles from the front-line town of Osijek where the low-level Serbian-Croatian war simmered on — now and then red bursts of explosions flashed on the horizon and you heard the distant thunder of artillery.

Pulling into Gašinci, I thought I knew what to expect there, for back at the end of the sixties, with my parents and sisters, I'd spent a year in the refugee camps of Austria. A long stretch of our stay there saw us in Traiskirchen, the tough and foul *Flüchtlingslager* where, only a couple of years earlier, Kratochvíl had slept with a heavy lock in his palm.

While I was in Traiskirchen, I pretty much liked the camp — there was no school and you had all the time in the world for sports, girls, chess, books, and trouble-making. I was learning how to kiss and how to shoplift; I was picking up German and realizing that to speak another language was to view the world differently; and I was maturing in a hurry as I watched the adults around me struggle with stress, guilt, anger, and lust.

It was only later, when I looked back on the camp over my type-writer while writing *The Willys Dream Kit*, that Traiskirchen suddenly seemed a pretty rough place — and there *had* been bloody knife-fights in the hallways there, and bedbugs, and seventy people crammed into a dormitory the size of a classroom, and inedible food, and management on the take . . .

While I lived with them, I'd taken all these things in stride, but as soon as I began writing about them a decade later, the First Law of Narration blew them up into a Storm of Anguish and Torment in the Black Night of Civility, but then another ten years passed, and I took a short walk around the Gašinci refugee camp and realized that my stint in the old Austrian *Flüchtlingslager* had been a Nap Under a Blooming Linden Tree after all.

INVISIBLE MEN

Gašinci had once been a boot camp of the Yugo army, but now it was a *lager* housing about two thousand Muslim women, children, and old men. These bottom-shelf victims of the Yugoslav war had all been "ethnically cleansed" from their homes in Bosnia by the Serbs and had no resources, no friends or relatives, no connections, no education — they desperately needed for someone to notice their plight and the Croatian commander of the camp gladly gave us the run of his institution: "You are welcome, my friend. Make all photographing anywhere. Anything you like, my friend."

The camp spread over a muddy hillside, dotted with ancient oaks. There were some forty unheated barracks and three hundred walk-in khaki tents — in the barracks, the lucky refugees slept on long communal beds, sixty or seventy bodies stacking up like logs under crisscrossing laundry lines. The more recent arrivals had to make do in the drippy tents where they slept on army stretchers a few inches above cold cement platforms — it was clear that some of the old people and small kids weren't going to make it through the coming winter there, but they had nowhere else to go.

I tagged along with Kratochvíl who only knocked on a barrack door after he had opened it — the refugees would stop everything and stare at him for a moment, but he came across as the Flamboyant Fat Man, a comical figure, so they smiled and relaxed again. Kratochvíl asked no permissions. Wearing a friendly grin, he ambled through the barren room and took in the atmosphere. He figured out the light conditions and, slowly, began to lift the camera to his eye. The refugees never became self-conscious, never protested, never posed — a few minutes later, life in the barrack was back to normal and Kratochvíl the Mellow Comical Smiling Figure was snapping up true images of barefoot kids chasing each other around the communal beds, leaping over the bodies of the women, who were trying to sleep away their depression.

While the pitiful refugees didn't mind being photographed by the Flamboyant Fat Man, I could sense they resented being looked at by me — somehow I was making them feel self-conscious. Could they sense how familiar the *lager* looked? Could they feel it resonate in me? Could they tell that I too had shuffled in the long lines in the mess hall, where the dinner consisted of two wilted hot dogs and a slice of bread?

I understood what it felt like to sit all day by the gate and wait for word about a transport to anywhere; I too had spent long hours in a canteen where ten-year-old boys waved stolen cigarettes in the wizened faces of old men asking for a light; I too had listened to incomprehensible announcements on the crackling PA system, read by giggling teenage girls while someone was squeezing their knees; I too had watched the sharpies in the mothballed barracks of the aid organizations scurry when a charity shipment came in — and now I felt guilty staring at these poor people and wanted to run and take down their names and promise that, if Kratochvíl's pictures ever came out, we'd love to send them a few prints . . .

The refugees sensed the turmoil inside me and they resented it: it was as if I were shoving a mirror in their faces while they were trying to forget themselves, which they did as soon as they set their eyes on Antonín. And so while, on a city street, Kratochvíl the Flamboyant Fat Man had a way of making me invisible, in Gašinci he knew how to use me as his foil, how to make himself invisible behind me.

CARTON OF MILK CHOCOLATE

It was our last evening in Gašinci and the camp administration had roused itself to a little PR gesture: Antonín and I were leaving the camp when a guard showed up with a cardboard carton and, smiling for Kratochvíl's camera, proceeded to pass out something to the refugees milling around the gate — a minute later, he was pinned against a barrack wall by a screaming pack of people.

The stuff turned out to be milk chocolate, thin, pocket-sized tablets of it — free chocolate brought refugees swarming in from all directions, pulling on their sweaters, hopping on one foot while pulling the other boot on. Shrieking kids were climbing up each other's backs and ripping chocolates out of any hand they saw; women were shoving one another out of the way and ramming chocolate inside their bras; a young mother plunged straight into the elbowing fray with a crying infant on her hip . . .

The crowd scared the hell out of the guard: at first, still conscious of Kratochvíl's camera, he struggled to hold on to his carton, but finally he just dumped the whole thing, and ran from the screeching octopus of outstretched, grabbing, clawing hands — yet all the while, right in the eye of the stampeding mob, anchoring the boiling mass of limbs with his big body and working the lens on his clicking camera with his nimble fingers, there was Antonín Kratochvíl, perfectly invisible to everyone but myself, with a couple of the priceless *lager* chocolates in his pocket.

DRACULA, THIRTEEN SERBS, AND TWENTY-TWO MUSLIMS

Right on Tito's Highway of Unity, in the no-man's-land between the Serb and Croat positions near the town of Nova Gradiška, there was a bombed-out gas station. Among its wrecked pumps, in glinting drifts of broken glass, there stood a rickety table and eight grab-bag chairs. Around the table sat eight men and talked and laughed and drank beer, courteously pouring it for each other from tall brown bottles.

These men shared memories and roots: the oldest person at the table had once been a professor at the local high school and the two youngest guys had been his students, but the professor was a Serb, the students were Croats, and that afternoon of beer-drinking in the ruins of the gas station was no picnic — the four Serbs and four Croats were haggling over human merchandise. They were deciding the fate of twenty-two other people, mostly young and middle-aged men, who were crammed into a blue van parked nearby.

The van passengers couldn't bear to look you in the eye — they'd glance up and, if they saw you peering at them, they'd immediately look away. A couple of them were chain-smoking hungrily as if they hadn't seen cigarettes in weeks; one older man's face was out of control with ticks; the sallow-faced youth by the back door kept opening it to spit blood — the passengers were all Muslims whom the Serbs had collected in Bosnia and they had clearly gone through something horrible.

At the rickety table, the Serbs were offering these Muslims to the Croats, demanding Serbian prisoners of war in return. The Croats wouldn't hear of it. They felt overwhelmed with Muslim refugees, and would only swap prisoners of war for other prisoners of war, though they did offer to take the Muslims off the Serb hands, purely as a humanitarian gesture: if you were a Muslim in the old Yugoslavia, your life wasn't cheap — it had no value at all.

The young man who had brought me to the gas station was a junior member of the Croatian negotiating team. He didn't have a big say in the protracted banter and, growing bored with it, soon drifted to my side. He was twenty-two years old and had recently been promoted to colonel in the Croatian Army. He wasn't allowed to wear his uniform here, though, so he had on a DEATH FORCE T-shirt. His *nom de guerre* was Dracula, but he felt ashamed of it — his face had turned beet red when his commander had introduced him that way.

Before the war, Dracula had hauled vegetables to Hungary in a truck, but when the war broke out, he discovered he was a great shot with the machine gun — earlier that afternoon, he had shown me a stop sign a quarter of a mile away and said: "if that is enemy, he is my." Now he asked me with a wide, shit-kicking grin on his face. "You want I show you one thing? Follow, please . . ."

He led me around the ruins of the gas station and pointed out a farm house a mile away which overlooked the Highway of Unity: "There, one Serb sniper, very good sniper . . . Kill my good friend . . ." I stopped to look, then realized this had only been an offhand remark: Dracula was already disappearing into some stairwell at the back of the station. I jogged after him, down the steps into a dark basement, and entered a pool of acrid odor. In the darkness, the Croatian colonel was standing still by the far wall, contemplating something, but when my eyes tuned into the twilight, all I saw there were some faded stains on the wall. "Here we kill thirteen Serb guys," Dracula finally informed me — he didn't sound gleeful or remorseful, just matter-of-fact. "I know some of them from before . . . War is bad, no?"

His words stirred up the sickening stink: suddenly, death was everywhere, it was creeping inside me too, invading my lungs; I spun around and made for fresh air.

Dracula looked pensive as he ambled back to sip beer with his old professor and his commander, but the negotiations went nowhere. Finally, an elderly Serb angrily slammed the back door of the blue van shut, locked it, and climbed inside. I watched him start the engine: was he transporting all those Muslims alone? Weren't there some armed guards coming with him? How hard could it be for twenty-two people to overpower one old man, swing the van around, and race for Croatia? Who could possibly stop them? Or had the Serbs kept the families of these Muslims as hostages? Would the Croats just return the Muslims right back to the Serbs to maintain good, neighborly relations? How could anyone be sure of anything here? How long before the slaughter in the basements resumed? Who could understand this war? How did that warm beer taste anyway?

The old Serb had nothing to worry about. He drove right past me as he pulled out of the gas station and I caught a glimpse of the Muslims sardined inside his van — they were openly crying now, grown men, terrified, broken.

I watched the van roll slowly down the empty and desolate Highway of Unity, saving precious gasoline, getting smaller in the pall of dark smoke, for they were burning Croatian farms on the Serbian side, watched it come and go in the black fumes, and there was not a damn thing I could do about it, or about anything else here, and it made me feel like shit.

BOOK
OF
MOMENTS

GRACE

It was a peaceful moment under a big sky when you wanted time to stop — in the platinum sunlight, you could see a hundred kilometers of the soft folds of the worn Earth at the center of old Europe. The wind was whistling softly, a melody to the pianissimo rhythms of water rushing everywhere, for the last snows of winter were thawing in the Krkonoše Mountains.

I was looking down a huge meadow sloping to a pocket-sized pine forest. It was strewn with shawls of mountain flowers and rugs of grasses, covering all the shades of the color of paradise, from yellow-green to blue-green, and stitched together by dipping threads of silver streams. Way down in the sea of grass, in the warm sunshine, two tiny kids were building dams, jumping over the creeks to get more sticks and springing back and busting the dams again. I couldn't hear them, but I read their excitement in the movements of a big gray dog, bouncing around as if he were a fluffy weight attached to them by an invisible leash.

The kids had the gift of grace in the way they moved and they were barely conscious of the dog — the world had dropped away and there was just the water rushing down the green mountain, the clear cold water that only a little while ago had been white snow.

BUCKET OF ACID

I was signing books in an overheated bookstore. She was about forty, plain-looking, with a nice, shy smile. She had bought all three of my books — our brief exchange was my Czech Generic Book-Signing Conversation Piece. "Did you want me to inscribe this book to anybody?" I asked her.

"Oh, no!" she panicked.

"Well, is this a gift?"

"No, no . . ."

"Well, why don't I inscribe it to you then?"

"That's all right."

Everyone in the line that snaked around the room was looking at her now and she just wanted to cut and run. "Come on! What's your name? It'll run you the same money," I said, because I enjoyed talking to people and figured these folks had come here to check me out anyway.

"Well, you could put down 'for Jarmila' if you wanna . . ."

I put my pen to the paper: "So is it Miss Jarmila?"

"Miss?! Are you kidding me?" she finally warmed up, and I wrote a personal dedication into all three books and she walked away beaming: the Czechs loved to make a connection, but they were terrified of looking stupid. They rarely blurted out something just because they couldn't contain themselves — Prague ran on the Five-Second Self-Consciousness Delay.

I'd forgotten this was what I'd grown up with as a kid, forgotten the burning humiliation I'd felt over things that an American might barely have noticed in passing, forgotten this was how it had always been in Prague, where shame was still stalking you with a bucket of acid — and when I realized it, I missed Chicago, missed people whooping and hollering and asking dumb questions, missed hearing weekend jocks give pep talks to themselves, missed watching baseball millionaires beg their bats for a hit on national television, and I wanted to go back to America and be surrounded by people at ease.

BIG CITY

I was driving Sonja to her modern gymnastics class. She was strapped into the passenger seat beside me, holding the pink hula hoop, the pink jump rope, and the pink ball on her lap, and taking everything in with her big eyes. I was making a right-hand turn when, out of the corner of my eye, I caught a glimpse of an elderly man in another *Favorit* making some sort of a gesture at me.

I glanced over at him again at a red light down the street: he seemed to be swearing at me. I had no idea what his beef was, so I pumped my head to say, Whattaya want, old man? He ripped his door open and tore out of the car, roaring at the top of his lungs: "You son of a bitch, don't you know how to flip a turn signal, you ass-hole?!" He was over sixty, crimson in the face, courting a heart attack in a big way.

"Dad? What was wrong with that guy?" my six-year-old asked, earnestly puzzled — I didn't know how to explain to her the Sheer Mad Slashing Artery-Popping Fury that would keep building in you if, all your life, under the bucket of acid, you had flipped the turn signal every time.

DAD, CAN YOU TRANSLATE?

It was a perfect day for soccer near the end of the summer of 1992, before our kids had started their Czech school.

"What does *píča* mean, dad?" Adam had asked me, trying to understand the chant of the youths with the flags, the jerseys, and the painted faces.

I pretended I hadn't heard the question — I'd already translated the chants of "you ain't shit!" hurled at the visiting team and the chant of "black swine, black swine, black swine," aimed at the referee, but now this referee had called back a dubious goal by the home team.

"Dad? What're they saying?" Adam insisted — I wanted to tell him that, twenty-five years ago, when I'd gone to soccer games in Prague with my Dad, you never heard language like this, that the pathology was rising sharply in Prague too, but that if you lived in a shame-driven culture, maybe this wasn't such a bad way to release your frustrations . . .

"Dad? I'm trying to learn Czech, all right? Can't you help me?"

"The ref is a cunt," I translated the chant, staring down on the field.

"Oh," said my nine-year-old and he too was suddenly captivated by the soccer ball bouncing harmlessly around the midfield.

PUTSCHISTS AND BODY GUARDS

The party in the back room of a smoky greasy spoon was in full swing — I was turning forty, Joska Skalník was turning forty-five, and we were celebrating our birthdays together next door to his studio. The joint was called Bohouš' Pub and it opened early in the morning for all the guys in overalls who drank their breakfasts, then filled up at noon with all the guys in shirts who drank their lunch.

The party was a great success — there were witty toasts, funny poems, great interpretations of the "Happy Birthday" tune, one of them blown into a tiny pipe through a nose. There was headcheese and tripe soup and soft, fragrant bread and horrible Czech sugar-cured wine and terrific Czech beer and no one was feeling any pain by the time a spasm of commotion seized the front room — President Václav Havel had just come in.

My family got very excited to shake hands with a Real-Life Life-Sized Live Linear-Reality Art-Is-Elsewhere President, but the personnel of Bohouš' Pub were unimpressed: the bar had once been an Old Underground Hang-Out and the waiters all knew Havel back when folks would have laughed if you had told them that this shy, bookish man was going to become their Commander in Chief.

Havel had been invited by Joska, but he was bringing a bunch of uninvited guests with him. "Would it be okay if these guys here crash the party?" the president asked with his signature politeness.

The party-crashers were all faces off the TV set: one Zielenec the Minister of Foreign Affairs, one Kočárník the Minister of Finance, and one Kalvoda the Deputy Prime Minister — I didn't throw many parties, had no social ambitions whatsoever, but this was ridiculous.

It took Havel's former body guard, John Bok, to put these late arrivals into perspective. As the president was seating his subdued ministers beside a row of lurid one-arm bandits and ordering them a beer, Bok marched up to Joska and barked: "Let's go do it, man! There's never gonna be a better moment for a putsch in this country! But Joska, you *are* taking that presidential chair, buddy, and I don't wanna hear another word about it!"

President Havel burst out laughing, but his hulking body guards gave up only Tight Little Ha-Ha Very-Funny grins.

PURIST

Maybe it was the way I walked in and asked: "Could we have that window table?" The headwaiter blocked my way, checking me over from head to toe. He had greasy hair and a Shiny Family-Heirloom Tux with Dandruff Epaulets, but he acted as if he ran a Nineteen-and-a-Half-Guide-Michelin-Stars Joint: "We require proper attire in here . . ."

I gave the place a long look: the dining room was completely empty and lit like a train station; the damask tablecloth was off-white; the flowers on the tables were wire and plastic; the waiters sat around smoking cigarettes — the place clearly lived off its proximity to Prague's daintiest church, the Loreta, which looked like a blown-up jewel-studded mantel clock. But it was winter now and Loreta's famous carillon had been switched off — we were probably the closest thing to tourists they were going to see here this evening.

"What's proper attire in here?" I asked.

"A dinner jacket and a tie."

I was wearing a leather jacket over a turtleneck sweater: "Well, so good night then . . ."

The headwaiter waited till I pumped the door handle before he spoke up again: "Well, maybe we could let the tie slide . . ." He was doing me a huge favor and didn't even bother to wait for my reply.

He glanced at one of the young waiters — this man wanted our business, for he jumped up and made for the cloak room, hustling back with a gray dinner jacket flopping on a hanger.

I hated those things: the sleeves never fit, the lapels bulged out, there were tiny cigarette burns or the stink of cigars — why should I pay to be uncomfortable? Yet it was cold outside and chances were the other places in this neighborhood wouldn't be much better, so I tried again: "Okay, look, maybe I'm not wearing a dinner jacket properly speaking, but this *is* a jacket . . . And since there's no one in here to see me anyway . . . Come on, what do you say?"

"We have our policy, sir" — the headwaiter was a Purist Who Went By the Book Period, yet there was more to his attitude than just the love of rules, which was a common passion in Prague: he was an older man who had gotten used to wielding unquestioned power in the Simple Old Days of Communists and Dissidents, when there never were enough seats in the restaurants. But I didn't owe Dandruff Epaulets anything and didn't feel like acting grateful: "Okay then."

The howling wind almost ripped the door out of my hand as I opened it again and Zdena gave me a look that said, Oh, come on, can't we just stay here anyway?

"I don't get it," I tried one last time. "No one's here, no one's coming, so I'd be wearing that silly thing just for your benefit . . . Do you care that much?"

But the headwaiter had read the wife's look too, and figured he had me: "I'm sorry, but that's the rule here," he said.

Well, maybe that's why this place is so dead, I thought but didn't say it.

The street was freezing — I glanced back into the window of the restaurant: the young waiter was giving the Purist In Charge of Keeping the Barbarians Out a piece of his Service-Sector Mind. At least Zdena wasn't saying anything.

WINGED CHARIOT

It was a brief moment when, suddenly, the *Favorit* went airborne — the feeling was the same as when you gun the engine to the top of a hill and then, just as you're flying over the very hump of it, take the foot off the gas pedal: the car leaves the ground for a second, your stomach flies up, and you feel a little slip in gravity's hold, the same lightness in the body you get by jumping up in a dropping elevator. This little car flight, though, happened on a level road.

The dusk was falling and I was driving through the spooky Krajina hills in Croatia with Antonín Kratochvíl. We were coming back to the only good hotel in the area from the bombed-out town of Pakrac. We'd had a choice of routes: there was the six-hour drive-around which everybody took, or there was this hour-long straight shot through the wooded hills, which the Croats insisted was absolutely safe, even though the road skirted the no-man's-land between the Croatian and Serbian positions in an area of fuzzy borders.

I was gunning the car down the two-lane highway which wound its way through narrow, leafy valleys — there could have been anyone or anything in the trees that squeezed the road from both sides, and my *Favorit* was a strange car here, with strange license plates, at a strange time when the Serbs were paying bounty for journalist heads . . .

The scariest part of the ride, the thing that really worked on the pit of your stomach, was the eerie stillness of the landscape. We hadn't seen a single car, or a person, or a farm animal in the quiet hills, and the road too had an abandoned look to it: vegetation was creeping in, junk was collecting on its shoulders, road signs lay toppled on the ground — you stepped on the gas and tried to make this ride as short as possible, but then you skidded out of a curve and into a split-second decision: a wire stretched across the road before you, some hundred and fifty feet up, too close to stop anymore at that speed, because you'd only skid right into it anyway . . . So you just stomped on the gas pedal again, the engine revved up, your stomach flew up, you sucked in a little air and held your breath as all the muscles in your body tightened — now the wire was under you — now the car was airborne — now time stopped, now you waited — you waited while the first stars were coming out in the sky — you waited now for the deafening explosion that would keep the car in the air — for the blast-off that would push you away from the Earth forever — you waited for the pale stars to pull you up.

LEŠENÍ

Right then I knew it was time to head back to the mortgage — we had been in Prague for almost a year and I'd started translating my American plays back into Czech. I'd lost my nervousness about writing in the language and realized I was probably regressing toward Czech a little, yet I remembered how gradually the Czech words had flaked off my memory and thought everything was under control. That afternoon, I was looking for a wine bar I wasn't familiar with on a sun-beaten street chocking with traffic. I was meeting my old high school buddies from the Provincial Town there, but I'd just walked down the block where the bar was supposed to be and hadn't found the place.

I hadn't seen these people in twenty years, though, and I was thinking back while thinking ahead too, so I'd probably just strolled right past it. I doubled back and looked more carefully — sure enough, the wine bar was right there where they had said it would be, but it was hidden under a . . . Screened by a . . . Wrapped in a . . . It was right under this, you know, this *lešení* . . . They were fixing the facade of this building, so they had put up this . . . This structure of rusty pipes and wooden platforms the construction guys tack right onto the outside of a house . . . You know, a *lešení* . . .

BOOK
OF
HOME

THEORY OF HOME

What makes a writer's home? A book. What makes the book? The words. And what makes the words? The feeling. And what makes the feeling? The clock. And what makes the clock?

REALITY OF HOME

Back when the Crimson-and-Gold Communism still had the future on its side, Libor Fára, a very fine Czech painter, went on a tour of the Soviet Union and discovered the greatest living painter there. The man lived in a tiny apartment in the warren of some forsaken public housing on the muddy outskirts of Moscow, but he made Kandinsky look like a color-blind, arthritic accountant — he had a glorious sense of color, an unerring feel for the essence of his subject matter, he worked on a monumental scale, and yet no one had ever heard of him.

In the messy kitchen of the Russian's apartment, suddenly feeling like a Sunday painter, the staggered Fára spooked himself by think-ing, What if they've got hundreds of these workaholic geniuses around here? Where does that leave the rest of us?

He sipped vodka and pondered the big, masterful canvases: where was all this power coming from? Was this guy working off the sheer bareness of his surroundings maybe? Had he been driven to put up something big against this desolate wasteland? Something just as monumental? And what else was he going to do around here any-way? Had there ever been a monastery as free of distraction as this place?

The Russian genius had a home like nobody ever had a home, but Fára was seized there by a sudden, intense spasm of love for Prague, the city where there was no reason to strain so hard against the world, no compulsion to be so heroic, and where life was full of dis-tractions, for weren't the distractions the best part of living?

A little more vodka, and Fára noticed that the apartment had a very small door. "It must be a bitch getting your canvases through there, huh?" he said to his host.

"Oh, I can't," said the Russian, "they're too big."

"So how do you get them out of here then?" Fára asked.

"I don't," the Russian genius just shrugged his shoulders, "Why?"

WHAT IF

The voice of *Reader's Digest* called me from Budapest, Hungary, speaking English with a trace of a foreign accent under a blue-collar American inflection. The magazine was setting up a Czech edition and needed an editor in chief for it — would I get together with them to talk about it? "Ya won't regret it," said Budapest, "they're good people, they take care of ya."

He was dangling before me something I'd been secretly thinking about, a notion I'd been toying with in my mind for some time: shouldn't we just stay in Prague for another year? Couldn't I support the family much easier here? Wouldn't a few magazine articles buy me all the time I needed for my own writing? (What writing?) Okay, but didn't Prague mean freedom?

And yet, the reasons to return into the Maw of the Terrifying American Emptiness were powerful and straightforward: Adam and Sonja had to get back to English, which was going to be their first language. They had to get away from the bucket of acid. And they had to leave Prague, for the city of operatic beauty was also danger-ously unhealthy — in Prague, where lentils swam in goose lard and muddy water could spurt out of the tap at any time, the soot fell like ticker tape. In winter, when all the brown-coal stoves fired up, asthmatics gagged; in schools gym was canceled for weeks on end; and there were even helpful hints on what to do if your children experienced sudden difficulties in breathing — you were to stick their heads out the window for a dose of the cold smog, taking care to put a stocking cap on them, so that they wouldn't catch a cold . . . Meanwhile Zdena was painting scary pictures and I'd had my *lešení* scare.

Still, I had to think over this opportunity carefully, for wouldn't a salary from corporate America amount to living rich in Prague? What if we could suddenly send the kids to the embassy school? Get a cottage in the mountains and flush their lungs out every weekend? Ship them back to Grandma in the States for the summer vacation? Get them tennis, chess, and piano lessons from the best in the business?

"Look, I'd be happy to sit down with you when you're in town," I told Budapest.

ARTFUL SIMPLICITY

Budapest, a slightly built Hungarian-American, came to Prague with Paris and New York — the two senior executives of *Reader's Digest* reminded me of the Low-Brow Corpo Lifers of the phone company that I'd once worked for in Chicago, the Fearless Leaders in Brook's Brothers suits who would traipse through my computer room and stop and cock their heads and stare thoughtfully at the hardware. The three Americans stayed in the hideous Internacionál Hotel and it was there they gave me a free Lecture on the Art of Writing.

"Artful simplicity is what we're looking for," said New York off his highest rung in the corporation.

"That's right. Most powerful kind of writing there is," nodded Paris the Amen-Sayer.

"Does that sound easy you think?" asked New York.

"Think again," said Paris.

"Absolutely," said Budapest and then he shut up and let his superiors handle me.

"I don't care who you are, I don't care how beautifully you may string the words together — we can take your piece and rewrite it with half the words and lose nothing at all of its impact," said New York.

"Make it a sight better in fact," said Paris.

"And then we give you that special kick when we tell you: this is a true story," said New York.

"And boy, something happens inside of you once you know: this has really happened to a real person," said Paris.

"We have more people on the payroll checking facts than anything else," said New York.

"That surprised the heck out of me when I found out," said Paris. "That's really counterintuitive."

"Artful simplicity in giving you proven reality," said New York. "That's what's made us the most widely read publication in the world today."

"No one outsells us world-wide, nobody," said Paris.

"You're a writer, why am I telling you all this?" said New York and then he explained the job: the editor in chief oversaw the translation of their articles and chased local publicity. He was not even trusted to choose compilations from the local press.

"Now does that mean that you can't be creative in this job?" asked New York. "That's what you're thinking, isn't it?"

"Doesn't mean that at all," answered Paris.

"Take our friend here," New York pointed at Budapest, "he just did an incredibly creative thing! He pulled all our old articles and culled the perfect story for his Easter issue."

"Is that right?" Paris was in awe of Budapest who folded his hands in his lap and checked his fingernails.

"Yes, it is! He went all the way to the sixties and found a story about Fabergé Easter Eggs!" said New York.

"How about that?" said Paris.

"Well, but it *was* a great story though . . ." said Budapest modestly.

"Yes, it was!" gushed New York. "It was a great piece of writing! And it was pertinent! And the Hungarian reading public hadn't had a chance to read it yet! What with Communism and all that . . ."

It occurred to me that maybe I ought to try and get myself hired, go through the couple of months of the *Reader's Digest* God-Guts-And-Guns-Made-In-America Corpo Brainwash in New York, pin whatever mines I had to pin to the chassis of whatever tanks they made you lie under, and then write a deadpan report about it, but then I thought about it for a couple of seconds and realized I'd never be able to pull off the undercover part of it — they'd know.

Paris gave me the current issues of *Reader's Digest* and, at home, Adam fished them out of the garbage can. He really dug Artful Simplicity: "I can understand everything, Dad!" But he had huge doubts about the veracity of the real life adventure stories: "This didn't really happen, right? Nobody's as dumb as this guy who sat on a mountain in the middle of the Himalayas and just waited for somebody to find him there . . . I'd try to go back, or do something, anything — wouldn't you? Are you sure they're not making this up?"

I never expected to hear from *Reader's Digest* again, but a couple of weeks later the phone rang and it was Budapest on a humming, squawking line. He was calling to give me the Happy News: "Well, so more by the process of elimination than anything else, we found our editor in chief in Prague after all." He mentioned the name.

"Never heard of her, but I wish her all the luck," I told him and tried to get off the phone, but Budapest rambled on — I didn't understand why till he said: "Ya know, ya have all kinds of contacts there in Prague . . . Would ya mind ta ask around about her maybe?"

"What do you wanna know? Like if she was a member of the Communist Party?" I baited him.

"Well, yes . . . And any other information that might embarrass the organization if it came out later."

"Like what? Like if she's gay or something?"

"Oh, no, no, she's married! We know that . . ." said Budapest.

"You want me to dig up if she's a lush?"

"Well, we would just appreciate ta know about anything that might come as a nasty-type surprise ta the organization later," said Budapest.

"Let me get this straight: you're asking me to snoop for you?"

He got off the phone with me in a hurry, but I realized I needed to get back to Chicago to see America as it was again, for I'd started to idealize it in Prague. Watching the Czechs struggle, after forty years of Communism, with the notions of the invisible hand and the open society of laws, I forgot that these ideals were rarely reached in the real life of the West, either — the Number One Print Publication in the Free World banged on the Bell of Liberty out front while peeping through the keyhole out back, and maybe what it all finally boiled down to was this: in the West, people often weren't what they said they were, while in the post-Communist East, in a more forgivable and tragic way, people often weren't what they thought they were.

HEAT OF A GOOD-BYE

The new bookstore stood on a cobbled street and an Old Glory was hanging out its second-story window. The flag was the size of a bed sheet and it was brand new, its bright stripes and stars burning white holes into the twilight of a winter afternoon, a sight that had been completely unthinkable in the Dear Provincial Town of Thirty Thousand Souls for forty years — it was on this very block that the beefy captain of the *STB* had grabbed me with a few fliers and dragged me off to the police station.

On this cold day in December of 1992, with my American books just published in Czech, I came back home to Kolín to sign some copies. A bottle of cold beer stood on the desk in the corner of the crowded bookstore and I sat down and I scribbled my name, basked in the glorious body heat, and played a strange memory game with people: they'd step up to my desk and smile — I was supposed to tell them who they were.

I recognized all my old teachers, but confused the Russian instructor, who had been a slim, young woman when she had played kissing games with us on our eighth-grade field trip, with a stout, elderly teacher from the earlier years, upsetting her to tears. I recalled all the faces, but it did me no good, for I'd forgotten too many names — some people looked uncannily the way they had looked when I'd known them as a kid: their skin had toughened and wrinkled, their hair had thinned out or grown gray, but I vividly recalled their features, expressions, and gestures from thirty years before. In my mind, they lingered the way they were now and I thought, had this place lain in a time warp? Wasn't it true in Kolín that, as people grew older and their choices took them through different stresses and pleasures of life, you could begin to read the order in the faces of the rationalists? The rage in the malcontents? The humor in the ironists? The defeat in the cynics? The liver in the alcoholics? The fright in the paranoid? Could these folks somehow still remain the same kids and unformed youths I remembered and saw in them? Hadn't they been affected by anything since our childhoods?

I discovered that my old home town was full of Naive Realists — I'd set the first half of *The Willys Dream Kit* in the Provincial Town and several people brought dog-eared copies of an older edition of the book, which had been published in Canada and had been a Risky Hard-to-Get Possession in the Simple Old Days of Communists and Dissidents. While I signed these dear books, their owners wagged their fingers at me: "You know, that bar is really on the *other* side of the river ..."

"Your Mephisto couldn't possibly be making a *left turn* on his motorcycle in that chapter about the Russian invasion, you know that, don't you?"

It was no use pointing out that I'd written a novel, a fiction — did Mephisto ride a motorcycle? I shrugged my shoulders apologetically and was happy they had accepted my inventions as literal truth.

An old neighbor had brought an old black-and-white photograph of myself, age three, staring up at St. Nicholas. This Czech Early-December Candy-and-Fruit-Giver had on a mask and a mass of cotton-ball white hair around it and he was holding a tall white staff; I reached up to his knees and my expression in the picture was half awed, half hopeful, while my mother stood behind me and eyed me proudly, a pretty young woman in a room I'd long forgot. And someone else at the bookstore had slipped into my hand a matchbox with something sliding around inside it. I didn't even remember who had given it to me by the time I got around to opening it: the matchbox contained a tiny toy jeep, painted white — it was our old Willys Overland Jeep, the war-horse of the U.S. Army in the Second World War, which my Dad had bought in the mid-sixties with the money he was taking from the national bank, the white jeep in which we had once joyfully circled the main square of the Provincial Town of Thirty Thousand Souls and which we finally left behind, broken down, parked in a side street. In *The Willys Dream Kit*, I'd fixed up the old rusted leaky-roofed jalopy into a Joy Whisky Madness Co-caine Phantom Dream, but that was just an image in a book, a two-dimensional lie of a veiled autobiography — now I had the very thing back, garaged in a matchbox, as shrunken and diminished in relation to my life as everything else in my old hometown had become.

Back in August of 1969, when I left Kolín which had been the world to me for sixteen years, I didn't know I was leaving it for good — I never stopped and looked back, never said good-bye to the place, never felt completely done with it in my heart. But now, twenty-three years later, I'd sold, signed, and dedicated all the books my hometown had ordered, killed the bottle of beer, grabbed my gifts, and stepped out into the dark street — the Provincial Town was wrapped in its signature stink of chemical pollution, the American flag was flapping in the freezing wind, the Willys Jeep was rattling in my pocket, and I'd soaked up so much body heat from my old neighbors, teachers, and schoolmates I could walk straight home to Chicago, and I knew it was time to go now, there was no use stretching it out any longer, it was time, and I tucked my chin into the collar of the coat, leaned into the cold wind, and started walking.

CLOSED ON SUNDAY

The Airbus jet heading for Chicago lifted from Ruzyně Airport. From the porthole window, Prague looked small as it wrapped around its river, horizontal as it spread over the undulating hills, and so scaled to the human measure as to belong to a different century.

One year to the day had gone by since we'd arrived in the city, and sitting beside me aboard the plane, Adam and Sonja were now chattering away in a slangy, Prague-accented, street Czech, recalling their half-forgotten toys in Chicago — their memories of Prague could no longer be erased. We all had Prague under our skins for good now, knew it intimately and indelibly in its breathtaking beauty, knew its streets in their texture of flaking mortar and sunlit cobblestones, their stink of unwashed woolen sweaters and fragrance of freshly baked bread, their music of streetcars screeching around sharp corners and swan wings beating.

We had taken many long walks around the Lesser Quarter and the Old Town and knew how the light shifted through the streets — in winter, the city was pure *Gestalt* with thick fog rolling through the dark walls; in summer, Prague was an Embarrassment of Endless Detail in the thin Northern light lasting till ten o'clock at night: on overcast days, when every spout, gargoyle, rail, every drifting pigeon feather was illuminated with Grand Even Clarity, the ancient city spread before you as delicately as an etching.

We'd learned to move in the rhythms of Prague, found out how its dour Monday mornings resembled its dour Friday nights, felt the tugs of many *shems* working in the city and discovered that Prague had no police hour, no taxes, no bureaucracy that you had to fear, for Prague in the post-Communist Era was the City of Endless Possibility, still a place where river mud spoke, saints gave off blue sparks, presidents wore army jackets, kids sold lice, and the devil struck experimental deals . . .

The shrewd charmer that she was, Prague was making sure to leave us wanting more and she was still holding on to some of her most basic mysteries: after a year of paying bills in this city, I still didn't understand how her inhabitants survived — according to the statistics, the average monthly salary in Prague was five thousand Czech crowns (or some two hundred dollars) while our family budget had rarely dipped under twenty thousand crowns. And having twenty grand between you and the devil for a whole month felt like being flat-out broke, and I mean Boiled-Potatoes-With-Salt Speak-English-When-You-Ask-Me-For-Money Let's-Go-To-The-Library busted — how could the old people survive in Prague on fixed pensions of three thousand crowns? How come you hardly saw any poverty on the streets?

I never figured that out and, finally, gave up on trying — it was simply a Paradox of a Dying Marxist Economy, which you could only comprehend the way you understood the old Prague joke in which Rabbinovich runs into Kohn outside the synagogue. "So how's the old shop doing, Rabbinovich?" Kohn asks.

"Oh, it's gory, Kohn. Every day I lose 500 crowns . . ."

"But wait a minute, Rabbinovich! How could you possibly stay in business if you were losing 500 crowns every day?!"

"I'm closed on Sundays."

WHEN?! TOMORROW?

Descending toward O'Hare Airport, our plane banked around the Loop — Chicago was no Vapor and Dream, it was millions of tons of concrete and thousands of square miles of glass glinting in the bright afternoon sun, a bar graph of human ambition rising out of a hazy plain.

The Tough Vertical City of Hard Edges had a scale that made people look like ants and cars look like matchboxes, and yet I had missed it, missed the different colors of its people; missed its sea of a lake and its shoreline, the beaches, the sand dunes, the ice floes melting in its harbors; missed the Barbecue Whiskey Genital Heat of its summer nights; missed its blues and soul beats; missed the curt, punchy rhythms of its English. I'd missed the Inching-With-Blasting-Sirens Bustle and the Kick-Off Energy of the place, the grab-bag images and harsh music of it, the sheer Shut-Up-And-Show-Me Bullshit-Walks Balls-Out Vigor of it. And I knew now that once you had tuned your ambition to the pitch of this place, you couldn't sing your aria anywhere else: I was cursed with this scale for good, and now even to fail in Chicago was always going to seem more honorable than to succeed in Prague.

In the leafy suburb, a long-haired young man I'd never seen before handed over the empty rooms of our townhouse, but everything was in order. I moved our furniture back from the storage, plugged in the answering machine with the old message, and we slowly resumed our American lives, though it took months to work up an interest in what the newspapers and the television were reporting in Chicago.

You didn't want to know. There was tougher plastic, sweeter drugs, brighter marketing, user-friendlier infotainment — money flattening memory. There were more powerful guns, more lethal bullets, more reckless despair inching closer to our street. An eleven-year-old chilled a fourteen-year-old and was himself whacked for it by a fifteen-year-old, gang style, in a bleak underpass; another eleven-year-old with his ten-year-old buddy dangled a six-year-old out of a fourteen-floor window, then dropped him because the little kid refused to steal candy for them — more than ever, to live in the Efficient English-Enriching Energetic Enervating Exciting Embrace of America required a rubber neck and massive denial: I threw myself into the task.

For the rest of that summer, every night, I sat down and read Mark Twain with Adam and Dr. Seuss with Sonja. In the fall, the kids resumed their American education with ease. By day, Adam went to the fifth grade and Sonja to the second grade, but at night Prague kept drawing them back. "Boy, I hate it when I'm in Prague and then I wake up and I'm back here," Adam told me, recounting a dream he'd had about Grébovka Park around the corner from our old Prague apartment. He was sprinting down a steep slope in the park, going faster and faster, slipping out of control, and finally pushing off and soaring into the sky . . .

That winter, months after the school year had started, the kids sat me down and made a solemn request: "Dad, can we, please, move back to Prague?" They had clearly discussed this beforehand and were stiff with formality.

"Why?" I asked.

"Come on, Dad?!" said Sonja, "in Prague, school was over at twelve-thirty. And here, we gotta sit there till three! That's so long!"

"Plus these kids here are such tattletellers, it's incredible!" said Adam. "In Prague, nobody ratted to the teachers."

"And we had breaks and we could run around the classroom, because our teacher wasn't there," said Sonja.

"And did you see how many Moms there were on that teeny little hill when we went sledding the other day?!" said Adam.

"Yeah, in Prague the hill was much bigger and there were only kids there!" said Sonja.

"And now even Michael Jordan has retired," said Adam.

I lent them my ear and waited till they got their Prague homesickness off their chests, then tried to list all the good things in their

American lives — the bicycles, the roller coasters, Halloween, the oranges, the fireworks, the video games, the diving boards, the fresh air, the hockey sticks, the television, the roller blades, the air-conditioning . . . It was nothing doing: both kids yearned to trade Chicago for the Non-Tattling Working-Moms One-For-All-All-For-One-Latch-Key-Kids Prague.

"It's easy for you to talk, you keep flying back there all the time," Adam finally hit me with a blow that was impossible to parry: I'd had a theater play open in the Czech Republic and was writing articles about matters Czech — I'd been going to Prague so often I was getting my every other haircut in the old country. Most of all, however, I'd begun to write this book, which took me back to Prague every day.

Zdena had got a job right after our return to help her forget. She wasn't painting, but she was writing a lot of letters and listening to the music of Irena Budweiserová all the time — in the end, Prague had left all four of us feeling roughly the way Sonja had felt about her "nature school."

In the spring of 1993, for two weeks, Sonja's Prague class had transferred to a lodge in the woods. The idea was to take the children out of the polluted city, but Sonja was the youngest child and the only foreigner in the group, and she'd never been away from us — at first, I didn't know if I wanted her to go, but she talked me into letting her.

The parents were not allowed to visit the "nature school" and the two weeks dragged slowly. Finally, the bus with the first-graders pulled up to the school again. Sonja jumped off looking tanned and radiant, and immediately started to show us all the wildflowers and mushrooms she had picked. Greatly relieved, I asked her: "So how was it?"

"Well, I cried every night," she shrugged her shoulders.

My heart sank: "Oh, boy . . ."

"But I wasn't the only cry-baby there! No way!"

"I see . . . So you probably wouldn't want to go back there again, huh, would you?"

Her face lit up: "When, Dad?! Tomorrow?"

A NOTE ON THE AUTHOR

JAN NOVAK has written two acclaimed novels, *The Willys Dream Kit* (Harcourt Brace, 1985), for which he won both the Carl Sandburg Award and the Friends of Literature Award, and *The Grand Life* (Poseidon Press, 1987). He also co-authored Miloš Forman's recent memoir, *Turnaround* (Villard, 1994). He lives with his family in Chicago.

❋

A NOTE ON THE BOOK

The text for this book was composed by Steerforth Press using a digital version of Walbaum, a typeface designed by Justus Erich Walbaum in the early nineteenth century. The book was printed on acid free papers and bound by Quebecor Printing~Book Press Inc. of North Brattleboro, Vermont.